The Nine Veils

The Reputation of God & Our Struggle for Identity

Nicholas Matthews

Foreword by Billy Hallowell

WIPF & STOCK · Eugene, Oregon

The Nine Veils

Wipf and Stock Publishers
199 W 8th Ave, Suite 3
Eugene, OR 97401

The Nine Veils
The Reputation of God and Our Struggle for Identity
By Matthews, Nicholas
Copyright©2018 by Matthews, Nicholas
ISBN 13: 978-1-5326-9788-3
Publication date 7/30/2019
Previously published by St. Polycarp Publishing House, 2018

Dedication

To the curious.
The student and the accomplished.
To the hurting and the healed.

For who that ponder the riddle of life and all who seek the answer.
Those interested in identity and God's reputation.

To Sarah, Daniel, and Joseph. Liz and John.

To the teachers, lecturers, and companions who have
taught me shaped me and journeyed with me on this
amazing adventure we call life.

For the students who have shared the experience. Thank you.

With special gratitude to Aaron Simms, St. Polycarp Publishing House,
and Billy Hallowell.

The Lord bless you
and keep you;
the Lord make his face shine on you
and be gracious to you;
the Lord turn his face toward you
and give you peace.

Contents

	Foreword by Billy Hallowell	ix
	Preface: A Personal Journey of Discovering the Broken Heart of God	xiii
1	30,000 Sunrises	1
2	The Importance of Identity	8
3	Clouds	11
4	The Analogy of a Day	14
5	Clouds are Inevitable	16
6	Three Narratives, Two Kings, One Choice	23
7	Analogy of the Veil	27
8	The Nine Veils	29
9	The Tension Between the Day of the Lord and the Love of God	50
10	A Return to Innocence	59
11	Shadowlands	61
12	Dealing with a Polytheistic Mindset	63
13	Being Free of a Polytheistic Mindset	64
14	Segue Jesus	71
15	Why People Suffer	74
16	The Suffering God	76
17	The Modus Operandi of the Loving God	85
18	A Mystery of God	100
19	Getting the Question Right	104
20	All Roads Lead to Canaan	108
21	Canaan: A Failed State and Beyond Redemption	110
22	A Terrible Reality	114
23	A Brief History of the Future	127

24	God in Canaan	135
25	The Unsettling Work of the Holy Spirit	139
26	The Knowledge of Evil, and Leaving Eden	150
27	The Fence	161
28	The Broken Heart of God	168
29	Carriers of God's Character	171
30	Appropriation	173
31	The Renewing of the Mind	178
32	God's Spiritual Compass	180
33	The Dandelion Principle	181
34	Conclusion: Veil Free Living	185
	Bite-Sized Bible Study Guide	187
	References	205
	About the Author	215
	For More Information	216

Foreword
By Billy Hallowell

Who are you? What is your identity? These are just two of the many questions at the heart of the human experience — questions that have become increasingly difficult to answer in the modern era, especially as culture pedals us a slew of mixed messages that collectively do anything but set us on course to live out our best, most fruitful and God-aligned lives.

Each day we are up against a ferocious array of messages in media, Hollywood and through our educational venues that run counter to truth and reality. Meanwhile, there's an enemy intent on authoring a confusion that slowly erodes our confidence in God and His unending love.

Due to an amalgam of misfired cultural signals and the pitfalls of our human hearts, too many of us buy into a multitude of lies that push us toward relativism — mistruths that tell us that morals have no fixed or central base and that our emotional whims should guide our thoughts, actions and worldviews.

At the same time, much of culture is being dominated by incivility, anger and infighting. These dynamics have left us hardened due to their overwhelmingly frigid and unfortunate chill. Too many of us have forgotten Jesus' commands: *love God and love others*.

Meanwhile, various veils are clouding not only our vision of God, but our understanding of His plans for our lives and, more broadly, the natural order that He set into motion. It is precisely this subject that Nik Matthews masterfully tackles in *The Nine Veils: The Reputation of God and Our Struggle for Identity* — a must-read book for any Christian looking for confidence in his or her spiritual walk.

One of the most convicting elements of the book is the much-needed focus on the potential veils that could be harming our understanding of the Almighty. This focus on the individual is essential, especially as we each exist, live and interact in a confused and dilapidated culture.

As Matthews so beautifully summarized: bad habits and malleable judgement on the individual level can eventually transform society. In *The Nine Veils* he writes, "When we let bad habits rule our lives we leave ourselves open for the enemy. If done in isolation, a bad habit impacts the individual; when the individual is a part of a family the family is impacted. When the family is part of a community, then society is impacted. When communities form bad habits, whole nations can be impacted."

Again: who are you? Where is your identity rooted? Many of us are rightfully concerned about the state of our world, but perhaps too few of us are willing to look deeper at our own spiritual condition, allowing apathy to reign.

Many of us assume we will be around eternally, shuffling the subject of death to the back of our minds while living as though our lives will carry on without incident. While it's true that we will each experience an estimated 30,000 sunrises during our lifetimes, there are no guarantees that we will each make it to age 80.

Life is short, and we serve a God who created us, loves us, and who wishes us to be relational with Him, getting to know the Almighty in an intimate and transformational way.

"God is good," as Matthews notes, but are we truly living in a veil-free way — one that allows us to experience and comprehend the fullness of his goodness? Are doubt, fear or the inability to answer tough questions about God preventing us from experiencing him in the way he wants? These are honest questions that beg truthful responses from us all.

God isn't afraid of our questions, as Matthews explains throughout *The Nine Veils*. The best antidote to doubt and confusion is knowledge and understanding. Matthews provides you with that — and plenty more.

- Billy Hallowell
Director of communications and content, PureFlix.com
Author, "The Armageddon Code," "Fault Line" and "Left Standing"

The Nine Veils

Nicholas Matthews

Preface
A Personal Journey of Discovering the Broken Heart of God

This is a book I needed to write. It's an area where I needed to find satisfaction. My God is kind, compassionate, merciful, and he loves me. I hold a simple faith, and this simplicity has held true for close on three decades. Yet, there are questions that remain unanswered; there are accounts of God that seem contradictory to my simplicity, and there are accusations against God that can leave me struggling for an explanation. At times, I've been confused by the concept of God's love and the reality of life, and there often existed a dichotomy between the two.

I also write this book after numerous conversations with friends who, regardless of their spiritual journey have experienced similar thoughts, or have simply ignored some of the hard questions of life and faith.

Common societal thinking in many areas is moving towards a position where people regard God as an outdated fairy-tale with a sinister undertone leading to apathy or resentment towards God. This is far removed from my notion of a living and a loving God who is kind, compassionate and merciful.

Embarking on my personal journey of discovering God's reputation, I have a hunch that I'm not alone. I need to explore God and find comfort with the answer.

Would you join me on this journey of discovery? Maybe all the dots haven't been joined, and some of the joined dots remain open to interpretation, yet the line I've used to join the dots is what I know of the underlying nature and character of God.

Nicholas Matthews

Chapter 1
30,000 Sunrises

"At sunrise everything is luminous but not clear."

- Norman Maclean [1]

Demographers tell me I'll live till I'm 80. That's fewer than 30,000 sunrises.

Under each sunrise I offer a simple belief. God is love.

I attest this belief to be true, and it's a principle that builds a foundation of confidence. It's not a romanticised notion and it's not a position reached void of the hard questions and challenges of life.

Reputation and identity are key factors impacting each of my sunrises. They either impede my walk or they assist my walk. My personal identity is woven within God's reputation, and this is true for all of us. Each of us will hold an opinion on God, and this opinion becomes our personal reputation of God:

- We love God
- We reject God
- We don't believe in God
- We find fulfilment in God
- We're sceptical and confused by God
- We're hurt by God
- We find meaning and purpose in God

Because my personal identity is woven within God's reputation it's paramount that my view of God is clear and without any hurdles or obstacles. The agitator of our lives, the devil, has one aim and purpose: to destroy God's reputation and to crush our identity.

There are several tactics the devil will use to achieve this outcome, and this book focuses on three:

1. Our ability to **doubt God**
2. Our ability to **fear God**
3. Our personal sense of **entitlement from God**

We live unique lives and we encounter individual challenges as we develop our identity based on an understanding of God's reputation. Our challenges are as numerous as the stars in the night sky, and for this reason we'll identify nine spiritual veils that distort God's reputation and weaken our identities; these veils, explored later, are grouped into **Doubt-Based veils, Fear-Based veils** and **Entitlement-Based veils.**

The way in which we view God is the single biggest contributing factor to our ability to live fulfilling lives and to realise the full potential of our identity.

The more I consider God the simpler the message has become. There are two forces at work in this world, the forces of good and the forces of evil. Each force has a kingdom. One kingdom is built on the concept of life; the other on the concept of death. When reviewing life, history and all that occurs in the present, we associate situations through the filters of these two kingdoms.

When there's suffering, we know this is not from God. Yet, life can remain confusing. Many people hold the concept that God brings suffering as a way to mould us, shape us, teach us and punish us. This is not consistent with the values of life, however. God always positions himself at the centre of human suffering, and because he places himself there, it's sometimes easy to associate suffering with God.

This book aims to equip people desiring to progress their faith whilst engaging in societies whose experiences run contrary to this notion. For the believer, it empowers us when we grapple with levels of doubt on our ability to say *God is love* in each and every circumstance within our personal lives, and the lives of others.

This book discusses pain and suffering and offers a level of understanding void of any step-by-step guide. Yet this book is not primarily about suffering. It's about God's reputation and how our identities are linked to God's reputation. When God's reputation is poor our identities suffer. God is the giver of identity, and if we doubt the source of our identity we struggle to build and achieve confidence. Many people associate God with judgement and it becomes hard for anyone to achieve a good reputation based on fear and anger.

Pain and suffering run through the entirety of the Bible from Genesis to Revelation; starting with the strange abnormal feeling of guilt, separation and shame felt by Adam and Eve at the fall, through to the disturbing imagery of eternal anguish found in Revelation. Adam and Eve were expelled to the land outside of Eden and through this expulsion our history of suffering commenced, becoming intertwined with the human existence:

"To the woman he said, "I will make your pains in childbearing very severe; with painful labor you will give birth to children. Your desire will be for your husband, and he will rule over you". To Adam he said, "Because you listened to your wife and ate fruit from the tree about which I commanded you, 'You must not eat from it,' "Cursed is the ground because of you; through painful toil you will eat food from it all the days of your life. It will produce thorns and thistles for you, and you will eat the plants of the field.

By the sweat of your brow you will eat your food" [2]

We all suffer. Sometimes we choose the suffering, most times the suffering chooses us, and sometimes it's a mix of the two. No-one is exempt, and for this reason suffering becomes an area we need understanding and confidence.

The Bible doesn't shy away from the struggle of humanity, and the suffering we experience has already been experienced by God. In many ways, God loves us through the scars of a broken heart. In the Genesis verse, God is not just pronouncing consequences for humanity, he was prophesying his own experience of suffering. John captures this profound contract in the simplest of narratives

"He is the atoning sacrifice for our sins, and not only for ours but also for the sins of the whole world". [3]

Whatever we suffer, God suffers.

"Since the children have flesh and blood, he too shared in their humanity so that by his death he might break the power of him who holds the power of death—that is, the devil— and free those who all their lives were held in slavery by their fear of death. For surely it is not angels he helps, but Abraham's descendants. For this reason he had to be made like them, fully human in every way, in order that he might become a merciful and faithful high priest in service to God, and that he might make atonement for the sins of the people. Because he himself suffered when he was tempted, he is able to help those who are being tempted." [4]

My hypothesis remains simple. God is love. But what of the questions that challenge the simplicity of this statement?

- How to explain suffering?
- How to answer people who argue that God does not love?
- Can it bring comfort for those angered by God?
- Does it bring peace for others feeling let down by God?
- Is God a God of war?

These questions are real and these questions are hard. Against the backdrop of Joshua's conquest of Canaan, the destruction of Jericho and the taking of the Promised Land[5], which is amongst the most contentious of Bible narratives fuelling antagonism and despondency towards God, we will investigate God's love.

Canaan encapsulates a myriad of questions, concerns and accusations against God. Canaan happened 3,500 years ago, but what of you and me in the 21st Century; the areas of your life, the areas of your friends' and families' lives, the areas where you have a question against God or a question for God? Situations you find hard to fathom and situations where you doubt the existence or the appropriateness of God's love. Perhaps it's sickness, perhaps it's economic hardship, perhaps you've been let down by those you trusted. Perhaps you have a heart full of compassion and struggle with the never-ending tirade of 24-hour suffering viewed on news streams. Perhaps you've lost faith in a society that's turned its back on values you hold true. In an age of angry-politics and increasing global threat, how does love respond?

The sad truth is we all suffer. If we don't look for suffering it will find us. No one is immune. Some suffer through association. At the start of this book several thousand Yazidis had taken refuge on a mountain to escape persecution; oppressors seek them through association with the Yazidis nation.

Some suffer through poor life choices. Perhaps through a downward spiral of drug or alcohol dependency, perhaps through a history of turning relationships toxic, or perhaps through missed opportunities and the choices of others.

Many suffer through the sin of others; the pharmaceutical company putting profit ahead of research; the chemical company operating in locations where environmental regulations are not as enforceable. This list could go on for a very long time.

What causes your questions and perhaps your accusations?

We're invited to ask questions, and this book invites you to ask God your questions. Yet, it's important how we ask questions; as a student or as an accuser. It's important to develop our faith based on confidence and to see our relationship with Father as one of an open, ongoing and genuine dialogue. As we progress through this book consider your faith; would you describe your faith as Enquiry-Based, Question-Based, or Accusation-Based.

If you're not suffering, how can you help those who are? If you are suffering, how can you empower your suffering to become testimony?

We'll discuss the fundamental question *'why does God allow suffering'*, and ask if this question is even valid. Does God facilitate suffering? Does God tolerate suffering? Or does suffering simply exist? These are fundamental when looking at suffering through the filter of God's broken heart.

We'll look at God's love through the life of Jesus. We'll explore the lengths and depths God took to demonstrate beyond any shadow of a doubt that he is love. This will not be accomplished through exploring graphic details of pain and suffering, rather looking at the underlying principles of God, and evidence showing he remains relentless in his love and pursuit of us.

My approach in writing this book can be seen as three intertwined streams:

1. Confidence
2. Questions
3. Testimony

I'm no musician, but I do love music. I love songs that carry a story, that rise and fall in tempo, allowing the rhythm to achieve high density one moment before descending to low density the next; crafting subtle textures developed through several melodies.

The streams of this book can be seen in a similar light; confidence, questions, and testimony. Sometimes my questions overtake my confidence, most of the time my confidence rises higher than my questions. Over the years my testimony has developed into a solid bedrock of faith allowing my questions to be asked within the sure foundation of confidence. At times my confidence will take a hit, and like the rhythm of a song, it lands within the framework of testimony. It's this testimony that carries me through situations where questions and circumstances have created long shadows in my day.

I no longer question God from a position of fear, or entitlement, or even anger. I've learned how not to take on the posture of an accuser when questioning God. And I sincerely believe God is happy with my questions; it's through asking questions that God unveils his character and his purpose for me. God delights in sharing his mysteries

"It is the glory of God to conceal a matter; to search out a matter is the glory of kings".[6]

I invite you to join the discussion of this book, and to reach a point where we can confidently say *'God is love'*, and identify potential veils that rob us of the fullness of this truth.

The challenge of this book is achievable; it's a life of veil-free living with full confidence in God's reputation and full confidence in our identity.

The reputation of God and the struggle for identity is real and is often more important than we imagine, where the battle for God-given identity in the 21st Century becomes the single biggest threat to esteem and well-being. A trillion dollar economy looks to shape and mould our identity – self-reliant, self-motivated, self-made, the right connections, the right music, the right entertainment – the problem is that unless we know ourselves we will always struggle with esteem and worth. There is a direct link between God and our identity. Knowing God reveals our identity, and knowing ourselves is critical as we navigate a hard and broken world.

Chapter 2
The Importance of Identity

"I love you," says Adonai.
But you ask, "How do you show us your love?"

- Malachi 1:2-3 CJB [7]

Whoever falls in love becomes vulnerable at some part of the journey:

- Will she like me?
- Will he reject me?

It's the same with God. He is deeply in love with us, leaving him vulnerable to our rejection. A common analogy of our relationship with God is marriage, and within marriage comes strife and even relational breakdown. This is the same with God and humanity; forever God remains faithful, whilst humanity has a poor track record of straying, spiritual-prostitution, general unfaithfulness and at times, hatred towards God. We turn from God so many times, and reject him on so many occasions, and this hurts God. We catch a glimpse of this relational dynamic in Hosea. God prompts Hosea to marry an adulterous woman, and as the story unfolds we see Gomer repeating unfaithfulness and Hosea taking her back each time. And this is God's love for us; we mess up, he takes us back, we mess up, he takes us back. Yet, this cycle breaks his heart. In so many ways, God loves us through the pain of a broken heart.

The quote above comes from Malachi where we meet God speaking from his heart; *'I love you'*.

Adonai says *'I love you'*. A straightforward statement of intent, *'I love you'*; and this simple statement is met with the question *'how do you love me?'*

This dialogue is profound; a simple question void of a simple answer.

Should a loving wife, sparkles in her eyes, move close to her husband and whisper *'I love you'*, and for the husband to meet this offer of love by uttering *'how do you show me your love?'* he's not as much questioning his wife's intent, or simply struggling with a choice of words, rather he's giving a glimpse to his own identity.

Malachi questions how God's love is shown. If we're secure in our identity and not prone to wavering opinions we could use this confidence in God's love to build a secure foundation, but it's not always this simple.

If we read from Genesis to Revelation, it goes without doubt that we'd be sure of the answer. Well, maybe, and maybe not. I've read the Bible cover to cover numerous times in different versions and formats, yet I still lack a complete understanding. For a simple answer I pull out the beauty of John 3:16 followed closely by 1 John 3:16; the love statement backed up by the how statement. Yet the Bible is more complex than a few stand-out verses. How do you use words to describe an intimate relationship with a mysterious universal spirit? For over a thousand years, God spoke through many and varied authors to record this love relationship; over 750,000 words to help shape our understanding.

For just as many beautiful verses and promises, there are many seemingly brutal and shocking. It's not possible to build our knowledge of God just on feel-good verses; we need to develop a secure foundation that incorporates the tough verses.

Demographers say I'll live till I'm 80. 30,000 sunrises. It's the decisions I make, the actions I take, and the relationships I pursue under each sunrise that makes the difference.

As a child life seemed endless, the long English summer days would last forever. Now in my mid 40s life still seems long, but maybe not as long. The single most defining legacy I'll achieve is my relationship with God, and a very close second is my relationship with others. Where first and second are so knitted together it perhaps seems unnecessary to try and bring a hierarchy between the two.

In the fullness of eternity, 30,000 sunrises is a mere drop in an endless ocean, yet as a son deeply loved by Father, my 30,000 sunrises are precious and special. To maintain the beauty of this dynamic I need a clear view. Life is too precious to have a veiled view of life, and a veiled view of God.

Chapter 3
Clouds

"It was like living inside Tupperware."

- Bill Bryson, *The Lost Continent: Travels in Small Town America*[8]

I love clear-blue days, the uninterrupted vastness of the sky. I love the sun on the back of my neck and journeying through the day with no need for a jacket. I find the vastness of sky conducive to contemplation, with a clear blue sky providing an unhindered slate to consider the beauty of life. If only every day could be like this.

Perhaps one of the greatest views I've lived through is an endless sky meeting an endless sea with hundreds of dolphins in every direction. Leaning over the bow of the ship my wife and I worked on we observed dolphins playing in the forward wake of the ship, to the left dolphins, and to the right dolphins; hundreds of them. I've had the opportunity to witness many similar endless views only punctuated with whales, flying fish, penguins, and the mystical green flash of the setting sun on the horizon. I find an endless view intoxicating, it lifts my soul.

Clouds get in the way; they distort the sun's rays, block the horizon and reduce the heat. Bill Bryson remains one of my favourite authors; America-born spending many years living in my home country. He combines a love of history and culture to produce some of the most insightful and entertaining books covering topics as diverse as travel, science, and language. In his 1989 widely acclaimed book '*The Lost Continent: Travels in Small Town America*' we meet Bryson returning to his hometown of Des Moines, reflecting on the vast schism between the climate of Yorkshire and Iowa

"In Britain it had been a year without summer. Wet spring had merged imperceptibly in to bleak autumn. For months the sky had remained a

depthless grey. Sometimes it rained, but mostly it was just dull, a land without shadows. It was like living inside Tupperware. And here suddenly the sun was dazzling in its intensity. Iowa was hysterical with colour and light." [9]

Whilst needing to remain mindful of friends living in Yorkshire, there is a good point to Bryson's summary of a dismal British summer; *"it was like living inside Tupperware"*. Despite never living inside Tupperware, I get the point. You look up and in every direction a vastness of grey, a grey that doesn't come with the delicate contours of cumulus clouds; a grey that is uninterrupted, and never ceasing.

Clouds are vital. They provide the needed mechanism for water to be transported through our environment, they keep our climate working. Clouds fascinate us, they provide stunning backdrops to imagery, they provide much-needed shade, and if you're like me you perhaps spent hours as a child finding random objects in the clouds; a pastime known as *pareidolia*.

Clouds also provide a narrative to various conditions. Sufferers of anxiety and depression often use clouds as a metaphor for their state of mind, and support groups and health professionals may use similar imagery to ascertain the depth of depression or anxiety someone is experiencing. Phrases similar to:

- 'being under a heavy black cloud'
- 'the day is casting a long dark shadow'
- 'all around appears to be grey clouds', and
- 'my life resembles being under a thick fog'

When experiencing life under a thick cloud, it becomes hard to see the clear blue sky. During these times, the sufferer can be burdened by varying degrees of worry that feel physical and heavy. Uncertainty increases, heightened levels of hopelessness creep in, and the awful feeling of guilt combined with *'what-if'* and *'if-only'* scenarios build and perpetuate through countless hours of harrowing mind-tricks. The sufferer's perspective has become obscured and they need help.

Anxiety and depression are often the breeding ground of guilt, a force that becomes lodged in the sufferer's condition making it almost impossible to self-remove. In effect, they need the clouds blown away through the interaction of others. Escaping the tunnel of anxiety and depression can be similar to a burden being lifted and shoulders feeling lighter, posture to be straightened whilst allowing the individual to walk taller.

It's similar in the spiritual realm where God has called us to an uninterrupted relationship. Under the ominous heading *"An army of locusts"*[10] Joel delivered a hard message to a suffering people; Judah was experiencing an unprecedented level of national calamity delivered through drought, famine and the onslaught of a locust plague. Their economy was crippled and their food supply decimated. It was not a season of celebration and the people of the land were living under a dense thick shadow. Read how Joel describes this

"a day of darkness and gloom, a day of clouds and blackness. Like dawn spreading across the mountains a large and mighty army comes, such as never was in ancient times nor ever will be in ages to come."[11]

The Tribe of Judah were living under a significant and terrifying cloud, described as *'a day of clouds and blackness'*. Hope and deliverance were available, however, and the God of grace and compassion had not forgotten his beloved Judah. Joel continues this theme of hope and deliverance with a soothing promise that God *"will repay ... for the years the locusts have eaten."*[12] I've clung tightly to this promise through my Christian walk. God will repay for the time I've wasted.

Chapter 4
The Analogy of a Day

"Beautiful one day, perfect the next"

- Queensland tourism slogan [13]

God provides a wonderful promise that his mercies are renewed daily.[14]

The use of '*day*' as an allegory runs through the entire course of the Bible. Debate surrounds its full meaning; a day as 24-hours, or representing a 1,000 years, or a season, whereas 'the day of the Lord' becomes even less defined as a unit of time, and in Hebrews[15] God uses '*day*' to demark a certain age. Yet, by simplifying life into a single day and applying God's promises to this single day, we obtain a beautiful picture; a day full of mercy and forgiveness enjoying the full radiance of the sun as we harmoniously engage each hour.

I've come close to a few days like this, but really, is this sustainable, is it spreading false hope for the countless millions who go through each day in a survivalist reality. Many people have terrible days. I've spent time in Cambodia with a charity working alongside land-mine survivors. During this time I learned how arms manufacturers developed mines resembling a child's toy, where shiny metal shaped objects glittering in the sun are too much of a temptation for a child. Raising boys myself, the utter horror of this tactic is how children often drop to their knees leaning over an object before picking it up. Whilst in Africa I listened to a preacher share how this particular region of Africa was as a field *white unto harvest,* the only problem is, the preacher continued, the fields are littered with broken glass, spent condoms and all kinds of dangers for children.

The challenge to blue-sky living is clouds.

The Book of Lamentations presents a progression of poems focused on the destruction of Jerusalem; a collection of sombre funeral dirges, where we meet a prophet and his God lamenting the destruction of Jerusalem. The author doesn't leave us with destruction, however; he chooses hope and it's during this period of mourning we read

"Because of the Lord's great love we are not consumed, for his compassions never fail. They are new every morning; great is your faithfulness." [16]

As I wake to each of my 30,000 sunrises I can choose to accept this promise.

God's compassion will never fail me and God's compassion is *'new every morning'*. It becomes my personal promise, I can start afresh daily no matter how thick the cloud may have been the day before, no matter how many times I failed, the promise is true. I've been given the ability to live as though the past is forgotten, move on from yesterday's hurt and receive endless mercy. I can allow the rays of each new sunrise to burn up the lingering mist from the night before, and no matter how deep I've dug my pit, his mercies are deeper. This is a great promise if only I could experience this every day.

Clouds appear and block my view; they distort God's love and deviate my plans. It's simply inevitable that whilst living between Eden and Heaven we'll continue to be challenged. God knows this, and God provides deliverance on a daily basis. If Jeremiah, the author of Lamentations speaks about the beauty of the morning, Paul offers a promise for the evening

"In your anger do not sin": Do not let the sun go down while you are still angry" [17]

Jeremiah and Paul offering a very simple way of living. We wake to newness, enjoy mercy, and the day finishes with forgiveness. Whilst we sleep God pushes the *'factory reset button'* and makes everything new in time for our next sunrise. I would like to experience this 30,000 times in my life. If only it were this simple. Clouds emerge and impact our days.

Chapter 5
Clouds are Inevitable

"There is no such uncertainty as a sure thing."

- Attributed to Robert Burns [18]

Whilst living between Eden and Heaven clouds in their physical form and their spiritual form are inevitable. If we only acted under clear-blue skies we would be lazy and hungry. I doubt whether Jesus had 33 years of cloud-free living.

As we walk through the day we need to keep an unveiled view of God. Yet clouds do form.

How can we see without seeing? How can we experience the fullness of God through the thickness of clouds; with the potential to wrongfully interpret our knowledge of God, to differing degrees, through cloud cover? Our ability to know what is above the clouds when our view is obscured comes through faith and confidence. Faith to see what is unseen and confidence to keep walking when the pathway is shadowed. At times, it can become easy to lose sight of God.

It's during the times when we lose perspective that we make poor decisions, and poor decisions so often result in deviations. As is the case with sufferers of anxiety and depression, guilt and hopelessness, the dark clouds of life provide poor perspective.

By drawing a simple timeline of events recording humanity's fall from perfection to the present day impacted by pain and suffering, yet with a focus on redemption and eternity restored, this timeline would look similar to:

1) The Day of Creation
2) The Day of Temptation
3) The Day of the Fall
4) The Day of Evil
5) The Day of Deliverance
6) The Day of Security
7) The Day of Redemption
8) The Day of Empowerment
9) The Day of Eternity

This simple timeline presents a panoramic picture, and from an academic level, we see how pain and suffering are temporal; only here for a season, and were introduced by the tempting of evil and the falling of man, and how we're being led towards the day where pain and suffering will end.

However, at those times when bad things happen to good people who are loved by a good God, then our flow of logic can hit a hurdle.

'If God's a loving God why does he allow evil; why doesn't he remove evil from this world' is a complex and common question, where the answer often seems as complex as the question. Yet in its simplest form, the finished work of Jesus provides the answer. The complete works of Jesus extend beyond our framework of time; reaching the past (forgiving sin, healing the hurt, and breaking generational strongholds); resounds in the present (providing hope and restoring identity), and reverberates to the future (providing calling and purpose).

'Why does a loving God allow bad things to happen' is a recurring question being asked through the generations. I Googled *'why does God allow'* and in less than half a second, Google provided 118 million relevant hits, with the top five subject headers being:

1) Why does God allow innocent people to suffer?
2) Why Does God Allow Tragedy and Suffering?
3) Why does God allow the innocent to suffer?
4) Why does God allow people to suffer?
5) Why Does God Allow Suffering?

These questions are increasingly relevant in an age of information and an age where people question the answer, and where people are desperate to find their place and find meaning and purpose.

The word *allow* leans too much towards God being proactive in the bad things that happen; a more accurate question would be *'why does God tolerate bad people doing bad things'*. We know God is all powerful (omnipotent) and he's ever-present (omnipresent), yet his Glory in the wake of pain and suffering does not appear to be a global reality. Because of evil, a symbolic veil has been incorporated to the human existence blocking the glory of God; in these shadow-lands, evil appears to have a level of freedom to operate.

God chooses to continue his work on Earth through us and through the empowering and counsel of Holy Spirit. We have authority from God to complete his work, yet we also have the ability to block and otherwise ignore his authority and choose to limit our ability to shine, or simply not engage in geographic locations where the light of God appears limited and the headlines become hijacked by the seemingly unstoppable tide of evil. There are many places today where I do not see evidence of God's glory. God remains all powerful yet his choice of display (you and me) can remain rather weak and timid at times. Paul [19] writes about the concept of being rescued from darkness and into light, being rescued from a situation where God's glory is not shining to a place of light where God's glory is shining

"For he has rescued us from the dominion of darkness and brought us into the kingdom of the Son he loves" [20]

A closer reality is that God endures evil, rather than allows evil. To maintain the question *"Why does God allow…"* blames God for suffering and by using His authority He creates suffering. Take a look at these instances using allow:

- 'I will allow the workforce to dress-down this Friday'
- 'I will allow the prisoner a leave-of-stay to attend a funeral'
- 'I will allow you to get away with it just this once'

In these cases, the person either has complete authority to initiate these situations, or they possess sufficient authority to allow these situations to continue; be it a proactive response or a reactive response. When it comes to the authority of God I do not consider he takes either a proactive response or a reactive response to evil; he has rendered evil defeated. The victory belongs to Jesus, and there is nothing more God needs to do. 'It is finished,' cried Jesus on the Cross. It is finished. God does not ignore evil, he's not swayed by evil, and he does not approve evil or need to excuse its actions. I consider God endures evil but for a limited period of time. The one thing we can be absolutely certain of is this; suffering breaks God's heart.

Progressing this concept further, a more accurate question may simply be to utter *'why is there suffering.'* This question comes from a learner's point-of-view rather than an accuser's point-of-view, or from a position of disillusionment. The wording of this question lays no blame at God, yet acknowledges the existence of suffering. When we reach a level of confidence in believing God has come to bring fullness of life, and the devil comes to kill, to steal and destroy, and where we no longer fear the imaginary Terms and Conditions of these promises, then the structure of this question serves us well; *'why is there suffering'*. However, when the reality of this statement goes beyond the philosophical and impacts our emotions and fears; where those suffering are no longer unknown strangers but represent loved ones, people close and dear to us, the philosophical level will not suffice. There does need to be a comprehensive understanding of suffering, and we do need the comfort of Holy Spirit when we're at our weakest.

Somewhere along the journey of eternity we will, I'm sure, find answers to our individual questions; specific events that remain shrouded in mystery. Yet, we do need a workable understanding today, so as to defend our faith against groups engaged in opposing the knowledge of God's character, whilst bringing hope to the hopeless and to progressively champion our faith in all spheres of society. God is good, and he has asked us to make this known.

Despite the fullness of God's love and the fullness of the price he paid for us, there are times on the journey of life where the actions and motives of God remain mysterious. I've experienced many of these times.

Several years ago my family and I walked through one of our toughest challenges. On the scale of human suffering, it really was mild, yet for us it was significant.

Early December 2008 is one of those times we'll never forget. We'd started the day in good spirits; the kids were at school and we had some precious time to sit, dream, and plan for Christmas. As a family we love this time of year; the Christmas events, the lights, the food, and the music. It was the start of a much anticipated joyous season. By midday, however, our bubble had not only popped, but it had been ruptured into fragments upon receiving a letter from Immigration. The letter informed us that we'd lost our long battle to remain in Australia and now had 28-days to leave the country.

It's interesting how human emotions can take us to such a high one minute and then bring us crashing to such a low the next minute.

Christmas was on hold. 28 days meant 28 days, there would be no more advocacy and no more prayers for an eleventh-hour reprieve. The decision from Immigration was final. 28 days took us to New Year Eve, and seasonal joy was gone, replaced with increasing levels of urgency looking for a plan. Where could we go? We needed to pack up home, and plan flights, whilst trying not to disappoint the boys by cancelling Christmas. We were 10,000 miles from our original home and being evicted from our temporary home. The only direction we sensed from God was to remain as geographically close to Australia as we possibly could, and the options soon became The Pacific or New Zealand. We had options, but also further challenges as travelling on one-way tickets without return-visas does raise border-control challenges. After many long and honest conversations with travel agents and Government departments, and questions and delays at check-in where manuals and supervisors were called upon, we were finally welcomed to New Zealand. Whilst most of the world celebrated, New Year's Eve found us at the airport with one-way tickets and three weeks confirmed accommodation.

The following three months saw us move eight times in six houses, in five towns before settling in one place for the next three months. In many ways, we had become disheartened and downcast.

Not knowing what God is doing proves hard, combined with the adjustment to home-schooling, completing a never ending tirade of paperwork, and packing up home every couple of weeks. Perhaps the most challenging part, however, was the uncertainty. We were staring at the 'how long is a piece of string' scenario; how long would this season last? Would we make it back to Australia? Days did turn to weeks, and weeks did turn to months. We were home-schooling and moving from location to location. For many years I'd suffered lower back pain, and occasionally this pain would leave me bed-bound. The five months mark proved to be the emotionally lowest point of my time in New Zealand. I was flat on my back in pain, mid-winter was freezing, and we were living in a very adequate but very low insulated mobile home. I staggered to the bathroom to shave; every step was painful. I looked at my face in the mirror and then glanced at the thermometer giving an inside reading of barely 1 degree Celsius. I was vulnerable, cold, in pain and felt I was doing a poor job of leading my family, and I became angry with God. I felt deserted by God, abandoned, I felt God did not care, and that God had become silent or disinterested. For sure, we could see God in our provisions, see God in the Bible, and see him in creation, but when push-came-to-shove and you're a father living out of a suitcase trying to protect his family, I guess I was expecting a little more. I wanted to hear God's voice for reassurance; have an Elijah moment, even Balaam's donkey wouldn't have gone amiss. But nothing. Finally, I uttered the words to God: *'if we were married, we'd probably be divorced by now'*.

Six months earlier life was going well. We were involved in leadership, new ministry opportunities were opening up, and Sarah and I felt we were in a spring season of life. Now, here we were, half-a-year later and I was angry at God, and even threatening him with divorce. I was cold, in pain and my hope for the future was evaporating by the hour. I wasn't happy with the person looking back at me in the mirror, and I was disappointed with the God I believed in. One Sunday we sang the hymn *"Whatever my lot, Thou has taught me to say, it is well, it is well, with my soul"* and this brought me back to reality. I had come close to despair but had come through. Close to accusing God, but saved from this. Close to giving up, but God showed me my 'lot' was light considering all things. I'm thankful for this.

Several weeks later we were packed up, saying goodbye to newly made friends, and heading back to our temporary home on a new two-year visa. In retrospect, I appreciate this experience and even thank God for this journey. You see, it was only in hindsight and with the ability to join the dots together did I see God's fingerprints all over the journey. God had provided the way back.

Our memories are now full of adventures, schooling on the beach, a time of family bonding, new friends, but most importantly of a God who cares even when He seems silent. Or, as the case turned out to be, of God holding us so close we didn't need to hear his distant voice because we felt his every heartbeat. We don't fully understand why we had to go through this, but we do have a testimony to God's provision.

Unless we have confidence in our knowledge of God's reputation, and complete security in our identity, situations can dictate our future path. Life does happen, and we do take hits. Yet, we can have complete confidence that God is with us, even in the mystery.

Chapter 6
Three Narratives, Two Kings, One Choice

*"Would you tell me, please,
which way I ought to go from here?"*

"That depends a good deal on where you want to get to," said the Cat.

"I don't much care where—" said Alice.

"Then it doesn't matter which way you go," said the Cat.

"—so long as I get SOMEWHERE," Alice added as an explanation."

- Lewis Carroll, *Alice's Adventures in Wonderland* [21]

Often simply summarised as *'if you don't know where you're going, any road will get you there.'*

As we journey through life we're confronted with three narratives. Two narratives are provided for us and one narrative will progress as we walk. The first two narratives impact our lives and lay the backdrop to two kingdoms; two opposing Kingdoms, with two authors. The name of the first author is *'Life;'* the second author goes by the name *'Death.'*

Both kingdoms have defining values and the means to communicate. The author of Life is pure and goes by the title *"Author of Salvation,"*[22], whereas the author of Death is known by the title *"Father of Lies."*[23]

We choose which narrative we live by, and by doing so, we meet the author of the third narrative; 'me' and 'you'. We interpret the world around us and this develops our world-view defining which narrative we tune to.

The hallmark of God's narrative would sound similar to; you are loved, you are wanted, you are pure, and you are special. The devil's counter-narrative sounds similar to; you're not good enough, you need more, you need to look different, you don't fit in, attain self-sufficiency, control your own destiny, and make a name for yourself.

According to which of these two narratives we subscribe to, we use our own words to create the third narrative.

Ideally, this narrative, our personal narrative, would reflect the Author of Life, yet so many times we choose a poor selection of words for our personal narrative resulting in claims similar to:

- God is angry
- God is judgmental, that
- God is a God of war
- God doesn't care, or perhaps
- he has more important and significant assignments than being concerned about me, or simply
- there's no such thing as God

We may once have believed in God's calling on our lives but now downplay this notion, and consider it more productive if God uses experienced Christians to achieve his outcomes. Effectively taking a position on the bench thinking we are serving God by remaining silent, and allowing a more apt person to rise to the challenge. In this instance, our faith has adopted the values of performance.

Many others consider there's only one narrative and this is the individual's, void of any spiritual input. This would carry the characteristics of a secular, humanistic or atheistic narrative confining God to obscurity and non-relevance, simply as a fairy tale belonging to a bygone era set in an age before we understood logic and reason and before science and understanding could provide the missing links in our consciousness.

Our narrative defines us, and it becomes important that we hear clearly.

Listen to how Paul encourages us to understand what we hear:

> *"There are undoubtedly all kinds of sounds in the world, and none is altogether meaningless; but if I don't know what a person's sounds mean, I will be a foreigner to the speaker and the speaker will be a foreigner to me."* [24]

In the perfect environment, we would hear the sound of God void of any distraction. Our proximity would draw us to an intimate position allowing us to hear even the very beat of his heart, yet distraction remains a reality.

Under each sunrise, we have our adversary offering a narrative based on death, lies and destruction. I often wonder if it would be easier to choose life if the spiritual was visible to the naked eye; the choice would seem obvious, or so I may think. Adam and Eve lived in this reality; they walked with God through the garden, they held conversations with the serpent and observed creation in purity, yet they became confused and desired something other than God to fill the centre of their universe. Why they chose self-determination over the fullness of relationship has been debated for generations.

What's important for the progression of this book, however, is the introduction of a veil to their existence; a veil causing their actions to contravene their purpose.

The challenge of our adversary is that he operates in the shadows and rarely makes a full-frontal assault. He deceives and he promotes doubt, apathy, and poor self-worth to achieve his outcomes. For those who consider themselves non-believers of the spiritual, he really need not pay a great deal of attention, simply continue to water the seeds of doubt and watch them grow. For those considering themselves believers of the spiritual, he will use whatever it takes to block a true understanding of God, and to filter our core belief in who God is. This will often be very subtle, and will involve our identity.

His tactics may not necessarily be to dissuade us of the existence of

God, rather spoil our view, and to make us unsure of our secure foundation. Something similar happened with Adam and Eve.

A person struggling in life through misplacing their steps and making the way treacherous for others becomes an unattractive advocate for the ways of God; very few would choose a travel companion who appears anything other than sure-footed.

Some years back my wife and I spent time in the eastern part of Morocco's High Atlas Mountains visiting the stunning geological formation of Todgha Gorge. Early one morning along with friends I thought it good to climb the rock face. As we climbed, the shadows were being replaced with direct and intense heat-rays. With little water we abandoned our attempts and started the way down. By now we were suffering and I was beginning to experience sun-stroke and before long I'd led a friend down a steep track to a cliff's edge. Although we were just a group of friends with no-one particularly interested in taking leadership, I had nonetheless led one friend down the same dead-end track. My delusional resolve had me peering over the edge ever-closer to the decision that it would be easier to simply topple over and see what happens when I hit the ground many dozens of metres below. Though I did retain strength over mind to avert this poor choice, I was nonetheless a poor guide for my friend.

Chapter 7
Analogy of the Veil

"And we all, who with unveiled faces contemplate the Lord's glory, are being transformed into his image with ever-increasing glory, which comes from the Lord, who is the Spirit."

- 2 Corinthians 3:18 NIVUK [25]

We have a great God, in fact, we have a fantastic God, don't let veils obscure this view.

The Bible makes numerous references to clouds and veils in describing the physical form and spiritual analogy; Paul uses the picture of the unveiled face as an analogy for freedom in Christ. The veil has great symbolism through the Bible. Under the Law, the veil provided a safety barrier between God and man; when we were not in a position to enter the presence of God. Under grace, Jesus ripped the veil that separated common man from God, inviting all to God's presence. The perfect sacrifice had been made, and no longer did we need the veil.

As we move through this book, we'll transition from using the metaphor of clouds to using the term veils. The reason for this transition is that unlike clouds, we can live free of veils.

The wearing of a veil becomes voluntary and becomes an instrument of choice for the devil. He encourages the donning of a veil so as to filter the fullness of God. Because the devil is a deceiver, the donning of a veil is rarely the result of an epic spiritual battle. Rather, it's more likely a slow and seemingly insignificant chain of events, and emotions, that subtly allow the veil to drop over our eyes.

We can start our spiritual journey with burning passion, and then find ourselves camped around the last flames of a weakening fire without realising the fire is dying. I doubt whether this picture, of a Christian drained of any heat with their backs turned against the world, provides much dismay for the devil.

An inactive Christian may pose little threat to the devil, where their fragrance has lost its sweetness and their narrative has lost hope. The Christian may be safe by the fire but their focus is shifted, they're surviving rather than thriving. Simply surviving under a rising sun is not what life is about.

It becomes important that we have a clear view, an unveiled view. 30,000 days to work out what life is all about.

Chapter 8
The Nine Veils

"Most people we meet today don't have a correct picture of God."

- John Maxwell [26]

If my defining moment is my relationship with God, it makes sense that I get to know God. I need to develop the right understanding of God through an unveiled view. The way we view God impacts our lives, our families, communities and nations.

For many, God is simply a fairy tale or a representation of moral and social values for the naïve and uneducated. To the sceptic and hurt, He can represent a war-God manifesting through the Conquest of Canaan, the Crusades, the Inquisition, Jihad and holy wars.

By declaring God is good and God is love, poses moral and ethical challenges for many, whilst touching a raw nerve in the fracture line of confused identities resonating in many of us. We think we know God loves us unconditionally, or we know we ought to think God loves us unconditionally, yet we're not fully convinced.

One of the more significant and symbolic imagery of God's relationship towards us is the veil; the veil that separated us from God. Jesus tore this veil revealing God and revealing the mystery of God [27]. We're invited to explore this mystery and to walk in free understanding of God.

When we consider life, death, the reason for living and everything in between; getting to know God provides both the meaning and the purpose.

I consider that we succumb to developing a wrong understanding of

God as a result of **doubt**: either we doubt all that God says he is, or we doubt he can meet our own personal circumstances based on our flawed identity.

When we allow doubt to rob us of freedom, this can ultimately bring in a **fear**-based perspective. We soon find ourselves interpreting relationship with God as one of reaching targets, and maintaining performance. Alternatively, we can personalise God to such a degree that, often subconsciously, we expect him to dance to the beat of our own drum and meet us on our grounds and provide for our requirements whilst meeting our **entitlements**.

Be-it the result of **doubt**, **fear** or **entitlement**, we can find ourselves wearing a substantial veil. We may still see evidence of light, but we've lost the ability to determine the exact position of the sun. We form assumptions of where the sun should be based on our former experience of looking at the sky but a veil has been put on, and over time the gap between our assumptions and the true position of the sun widens.

Veils come in many forms, shapes and sizes. Some are worn as a result of youth and naivety; some veils are worn as a reaction of fear and anger, hurt and pain; whilst other veils are there because we aim to mould and shape God to fit our own requirements, to create a personalised-God based on our desires.

The veil has been torn, yet we voluntarily re-introduce veils into our relationship with God. Nine veils have been identified and named, and once donned these veils provide a distorted version of God, leading to a distorted narrative. Through my own personal journey and walking alongside many others, I consider that each of us can relate in some way to the concept of these names.

Doubt-Based Veils

1. Absent-God
2. Performance-God

Fear-Based

3. Karma-God
4. War-God
5. Angry-God
6. Schizophrenic-God

Entitlement-Based

7. Happy-God
8. Genie-God
9. Safe-God

Doubt, fear and entitlement form the narrative of this world as influenced by our adversary, and they run contrary to confidence and certainty, faith and trust, honesty and forgiveness which form the narrative of God's kingdom. Moving from the devil's narrative to God's narrative is possible, yet takes perseverance and discipline. Paul speaks of this process as transformational in our lives:

"Do not conform to the pattern of this world, but be transformed by the renewing of your mind. Then you will be able to test and approve what God's will is – his good, pleasing and perfect will" [28]

Looking further at how these veils impact us:

DOUBT-BASED VEILS

Absent-God

Many people do feel as though God is absent in their lives, or that God is absent from specific events. A lot of this feeling, of God's absence, comes down to our ability to hear God's voice and to know of his ways when he seems silent. King David wore his heart on his sleeve and Psalms provides an intimate review of a man searching for God:

> *"Where can I go from your Spirit?*
> *Where can I flee from your presence?*
> *If I go up to the heavens, you are there;*
> *if I make my bed in the depths, you are there.*
> *If I rise on the wings of the dawn,*
> *if I settle on the far side of the sea,*
> *even there your hand will guide me,*
> *your right hand will hold me fast".* [29]

The truth is God cannot be absent. Yet he can feel absent.

This feeling of absence can manifest in many forms. We can feel as though God has withdrawn from us. We can feel as though God is absent-minded when it comes to our particular needs. That somehow he's forgotten us. We can feel as though God is a proxy-God, he cares, but just not enough to show up on the day. This poses tension for many people who do view God as a distant God, who would consider their relationship with God as a long-distance relationship.

Love needs to be expressed through a healthy relationship, and it remains hard to foster a love relationship with a God who can seem withdrawn.

If God is everywhere, yet he feels distant, we do need to look at our own positioning and ask the question; are we viewing God through doubt; through an Absent-God veil.

Performance-God

The modern world is increasingly driven by commerce and industry. In this environment, we become familiar with work ethics characterised by performance. Many nations have been influenced by the notion of a Protestant Work Ethic; an ethic closely linked to religious movements advocating for hard work and frugality as observable and external indicators of grace. We deliver on Key Performance Indicators, we implement 360 Reviews, we maintain budgetary controls, and we schedule performance meetings. We generally know our targets and we strategize to attain.

We've adapted to this environment, yet when we transpose this work-ethic to our faith we soon develop a performance-based spirituality and consider that our relationship with God is one of action and approval. This is not a new concept. Paul tackled a similar reality in the book of Galatians, the Galatians were using observable signs to determine degrees of faith; a type of *'faith plus'* spirituality. For the Galatians, this equated to *'Faith plus circumcision"*. Paul[30] writes that our salvation is through Jesus, not *'Jesus plus works'*, or *'Jesus plus keeping the Law'*, simply Jesus.

We are called to live lives that bear fruit, yet we're not called to build our faith on the ability to perform. Many people subscribe to a work-based approach, founded on performance and personal capacity rather than simple relationship. An intimate loving relationship between God and humanity results in a far greater breakthrough, and victory, than our personal capacity could ever achieve.

There's nothing we can add and there's no action we can take to earn more love from God.[31] It's true that our actions can displease him, just as the actions of any child can bring displeasure to their parents, yet such actions have not shifted love from its foundation of security.

My sons play soccer; I encourage them to attend practice, and I'm proud when they go on the pitch. Regardless of their performance, I remain proud. If they score a goal I celebrate with them, if they make a terrific save, I celebrate. If they miss a tackle or misplace a kick this is fine. There is nothing on the pitch they can do, or not do, that impacts my love for them. I simply love them.

Striving and being involved brings pleasure because that's the game they've trained for, and it brings joy to see them participate. They are on the right pitch for their training. Yet their striving doesn't buy more love. I consider this to be the same with Jesus.

Jesus calls us to fully participate in his plans and purposes for the world;[32] he welcomes our involvement and he enjoys our pursuit of the goal. Yet so many times we choose our own race based on logic by fitting our personal capacities with perceived outcomes. Or we may choose an area of service based on past performance, or what others consider to be our calling, without listening intimately to father's voice.

This does not impact Jesus' love for us, yet if we looked closely we may discover Jesus on the sidelines with a heart full of love but a heart full of concern as we've chosen a race that is not ours to run. We become tired, stretched and burdened. We develop tunnel vision and stop looking towards Jesus who is calling us off the pitch.

As this scenario continues we discover we're no longer kicking the goals we expected to kick; we start to hurt, and before long we voluntarily apply unnecessary pressure to relationships. It's at this juncture we become disillusioned with God and allow our mind to develop questions, and accusations similar to:

- 'where is God'
- 'doesn't he care'
- 'doesn't he know I'm hurting'
- 'I'm striving for him, yet he doesn't seem to respond'
- 'doesn't he know my life is falling apart, my marriage is barely surviving, and I'm never home for the kids'

We can develop theories that remove God from our pain, or, how God is causing the pain. Both perceptions are damaging. If God has removed himself, then opinions do form suggesting God is not trustworthy; if God has caused the pain then it must be a result of my performance. Worse still, God is damaging me and I'm his child, I dread to think what he does to those who oppose him.

Within a short period of time, we can form dangerous opinions and toxic conclusions similar to *'maybe God did cause some terrible event to happen because that's becoming my experience of God'. 'Perhaps he did cause that earthquake, or he did cause that war or he did plan for my neighbour to be struck down with cancer'.*

Performance-based faith may resemble:

- If I read three chapters of the Bible a day God will love me more
- If I rise in the early hours of the morning and pray, God will love me more
- If I burn the candle at both ends of the day then this will meet his approval
- If I give more, I'll get more

Praying and meditating are good activities, periods of labour-some work is not necessarily wrong. We are called to meditate through the day and intercede through the night, and we're called to persist and push through in prayer. Jesus modelled long nights of prayer, yet this was not to maintain indicators of performance. It was not a formula for success. Jesus prayed because of relationship. He loved those he met with an unfathomable love, and with full knowledge that lives are changed through intercession, we begin to glean an understanding of Jesus' motivation of spending sleepless nights on a mountain. He was relating with Father and loving humanity.

FEAR-BASED VEILS

Karma-God

This veil may seem misplaced, with Karma and Christianity being too far removed from each other. It's the transactional values of Karma that Christians can succumb to; a system of reciprocation determined by the level of good, or the level of bad a person has participated in. A transactional system.

We may not consider we've entered a transactional relationship with God, yet our thoughts and sometimes our actions can speak otherwise; God blesses the good that we do, and God punishes the bad that we do. This is reciprocal and transactional in nature, comparable to notions of Karma. Wearing a Karma-God veil, similar in some ways to a performance-based faith, will result in dangerous statements:

- 'Maybe God gave you cancer to teach you something'
- 'Maybe God's not healing because you have sin in your life'

Such conclusions draw on fear, are dangerous, and transactional in nature; God reciprocating good for good and bad for bad.

War-God

War is a conflict between rival parties for the desired objective resulting in a struggle, aggression and destruction of life and property. This doesn't sound like values from the Kingdom of heaven, yet many do hold the concept of God as a war-God.

The values of God and the values of the devil are polar extremes; God brings life and life to the full, and the devil steals, kills and destroys. This begs the question:

- Is it the character of God to start wars?
- Are there deficiencies in the nature of God where he needs to defend himself?

We learn the devil declared war in Heaven, and we see him defeated at the hands of angels.[34] The war in Heaven was a struggle between angels:

- Has God struggled in war?
- Has God struggled to maintain his Kingdom?
- Is there an ongoing battle between God and the devil to claim the Kingdom of Heaven?

Perhaps the toughest question really comes down to; has God been to war?

God is anti-war.

War derives from pride, greed and hatred; factors from the devil's side of the equation. Yet in redemptive principles, even war can be used to liberate, to bring freedom, and end oppression. God, through mysteries we do not fully understand, works through war. In our fallen world and through the confusion of hatred, we often feel the only option is to engage war as a liberating activity. Yet human war remains a man-made affair, a destructive reality made on earth.

People cite the Just-War Theory to justify war; a framework allowing nations, not individuals, to declare war in defence of their citizens, and the defence of justice. A theory where taking a human life remains fundamentally wrong; yet is a permissible but non-desired action protecting the innocent and upholding moral values. Many use Godly principles to rationalise for conflict within the framework of the Just-War Theory. The genesis of Just-War Theory advocates that war is always bad, that it's the lesser of two evils, but the practice of war remains evil. I do not consider God went to war only if it fitted within the parameters of the Just-War Theory.

The theatre for all wars is a broken and corrupt earth; where the factors of greed, hatred and abusive power fan the flames of war. Human stands against human with the intent of defeating each other through force. This does not sound like God.

Leo Tolstoy is a true master at weaving philosophical discussion around historical fact. The backdrop to his literary masterpiece; War and Peace is a changing Europe and a Europe in turmoil. Spanning the years 1805 to 1812 War and Peace observes the onward advance of Napoleon's troops across Europe. Ever eastward-bound Napoleon's massed army pauses momentarily at the western border of Russia. The confrontation between empires was, by now, inevitable. France faced Russia. Russia took position. Human faced human. Strategy and courage stood shoulder-to-shoulder with fear and uncertainty. As Emperor faced General, the simplest of commands was spoken, advance; one small word, one small action coming from, as it so happens, one small man seeking fame; advance. Tolstoy,

"Millions of men, renouncing their human feelings and reason, had to go from west to east to slay their fellows, just as some centuries previously hordes of men had come from east to west, slaying their fellows." [35]

The people of the west moved eastward and hideous loss of life and horrendous loss of morality ensued. This does not sound like God.

Every action God does is pure love. However, pure love looks different in varying circumstances. God has seen more, and been through more than we can imagine. God has stared evil in the face and has seen pure darkness and pure hatred.[36] When pure love meets pure evil, pure love will always overcome. Love in the face of evil will look different to love at the birth of a child.

What is God's stance on war, particularly as numerous pages of the Old Testament are full of war? Many people do view God as a War-God and cite the conquest of Canaan as the defining commentary to justify this claim; that God is a God-of-War.

I've had conversations with peers who oppose my opinion on this topic, stating the Old Testament shows God commanding war to achieve his purpose; that God is a God of war. Several years back I led prayer meetings for a Christian organisation I was involved with during the time of the second Gulf War, with TV screens full of Cruise missiles flying over Baghdad. This was an important world event and an area we needed to pray over. Yet, I became stuck. Some people were earnestly praying for the success of western nations, others were praying for the cessation of hostilities and the impeachment of western leaders due to illegal actions. These prayers were pure and they were sincere, yet they conflicted with each other. It taught me there are many interpretative approaches to parts of scripture, and the views of one dedicated follower of Jesus can vary to the views of another dedicated follower of Jesus, and it might be unnecessary to persuade for one opinion over the other. I did, however, come away from those times with a personal struggle *'how, on a matter as important as life and death, can we be unsure of our position?'* Is God for this war, or is God against this war. The only reasonable answer to satisfy my conscience was, and remains - war breaks God's heart. It always has broken his heart, and it always will break his heart.

War derives from freedom, the freedom of choice we received from God. When we blame God for war, this blame should not be the act of war, rather the provision of freedom. Freedom of choice is a decision God took; giving creation the ability to turn their back on their creator. The logical flow of questioning God's stance on war ultimately arrives at free-will; was it right for humanity to have freedom of choice.

When we turned our backs in Eden, God could have turned his back on us, leaving us to our own devices. But in love he chose to stand with us, acting as a dam-wall against the tsunami of evil anxiously waiting to flood the earth through an angry and raging torrent of hatred bent on our total destruction. Humans have the ability to tap into this resource and invite evil in. When nations and societies collectively tap into this resource, evil will have achieved a hold on society. Evil will grow and advance through society, breaking down the intimate relationship between God and his creation. Evil impacts the earth, and war is a powerful tool influencing the earthly realm mobilising and empowering humans to achieve these works of evil.

Paul[37] raises this reality of creation suffering through evil, groaning and awaiting liberation from sin:

"I consider that our present sufferings are not worth comparing with the glory that will be revealed in us. For the creation waits in eager expectation for the children of God to be revealed. For the creation was subjected to frustration, not by its own choice, but by the will of the one who subjected it, in hope that the creation itself will be liberated from its bondage to decay and brought into the freedom and glory of the children of God.

We know that the whole creation has been groaning as in the pains of childbirth right up to the present time. Not only so, but we ourselves, who have the firstfruits of the Spirit, groan inwardly." [38]

The Matthew Henry Commentary provides further insight into this predicament:

> *"Sin has been, and is, the guilty cause of all the suffering that exists in the creation of God. It has brought on the woes of earth; it has kindled the flames of hell. As to man, not a tear has been shed, not a groan has been uttered, not a pang has been felt, in body or mind, that has not come from sin".* [39]

The above statement does need to be read carefully.

As I write I have a sore throat. I don't consider my sore throat resulting from direct evil; rather it's a change of season marked by rain, high winds and cold; preceding a busy week at work. My body is run down. Yet, the ability for my body to be run-down and prone to illness has its origin in evil, where the choice in Eden subjected my body to decay and vulnerability.

I have close friends with late stage cancer. Cancer is a horrid thing where thousands of years of cell degradation have left a legacy allowing broken cells to group, grow and create abnormal masses within a sufferer's body. Suffering, illness and death result from evil, yet the seeds of this evil date back multiple generations.

Our understanding of death can mix emotions with reality. Death is our liberation. Death became liberation for Adam and Eve allowing release from their bruised and broken earthly bodies. Death became our way out, our freedom, and our onward journey to an eternity of perfection. Many people are angry at a God who starts wars, or of a God so far removed to even consider stopping wars, or a God who remains powerless to intervene.

God is not a War-God yet God chooses to be at the centre of war, as this is where people suffer.

Our enemy deploys propaganda to entice and destabilise. When we doubt our kingdom, if we doubt our identity we may fail to identify the difference between truth and propaganda. When this happens, the enemy has gained a foothold in a person's life. When society fails to see this difference, the enemy has established a beach-head, and if unattended, the enemy will onward march to the goal, and capture the heart of society.

The Conquest of Canaan and the destruction of Jericho remains a contentious issue providing the source of much anger and hatred towards God, causing discomfort for Christians, and rendering us ineffective in defending God's reputation. For this reason, this book captures my convictions – and my wrestling – on the events of Canaan.

For now, however, it's important to recognise this War-God veil. When we view God as a War-God this impacts on our interaction with God; it instils a fear-based element to our faith and blocks the true understanding of God.

Angry-God

We all experience anger as an emotional response towards displeasure, annoyance, and hostility. The reason we experience anger is because we're made in the image of a God [40] who experiences anger; however, there is a huge chasm between God being angered and God being angry.

- An Angry-God will display anger on ad-hoc occasions at levels that are irrational and misplaced. People living with an angry spouse, an angry partner, colleague or parent will attest to the unsettling nature this anger brings to relationships. It's a negative experience damaging trust and eroding confidence, where intervention by third parties is often needed. This doesn't sound like God. There is no need for a third-party to protect us from God's anger.

- A God angered at what harms us, however, is on our side. His anger is directed towards sin, evil, and the kingdom of darkness. It's a righteous anger and is always under control. This anger brings safety and security, and this anger protects those in need.

I expect Ban Ki-moon to lead the world in displays of anger towards perpetrators of hideous crimes against humanity. But should Ban Ki-moon become unsure of his position in the wake of evil, and if he wavered and turned a blind eye to injustice, there would be a challenge to his leadership, and global demands for reform. Anger is needed whilst we live in a fallen world.

Anger drives us to a response, and this response is critical. It is right that we get angered at the plight of children trapped in the sex industry, it is right that we fight against slavery, yet love needs to drive this response. This is the same with God; it's anger that rouses his attention yet this arousal is out of pure love for his children.

How we view the cross can be an indicator as to how we view anger in relation to God. By holding a philosophy where the wrath of God was poured out on the cross, we need to mitigate God's anger, and the cross becomes the instrument for this displacement of punishment. However, if we hold the philosophy that God's unconditional love was poured out on the cross, and we're the recipients of this love, the cross becomes a beacon of reconciliation and hope. Several years ago I attended lectures on the rite of passage for a Jew to become a priest, whilst looking at the life of Jesus as an enactment of Psalm 22. How we view the cross becomes imperative in our ability to share God's love with a hurting world. If we engage a hurting world where the cross is an instrument of salvation-from-judgement our message offers escape only, but if our message is one of the cross being the fulfilment of love, then judgment becomes part of the back-story whilst love is elevated through the narrative until it takes the highest place.

In the gospels we're confronted with harrowing words from son to father, *"Eli, Eli, lema sabachthani?"* (which means "My God, my God, why have you **forsaken** me?")."[41] Why did father turn away when Jesus died? What was going on when we read of God forsaking Jesus?

If we fail in our understanding of this exchange, we easily fall into the notion where God turned away because He's too holy to look upon Jesus who'd taken on sin; that the transaction of the cross was punishment based.

If this is the case, then how does God see us?

Can God even look at us? Does he rely on Jesus as a filter giving the impression of our spotless lives? Or could it be that, for a moment in time, God was truly devastated to the point he could not face the pain any longer? God felt pain.

If we consider God turned away because Jesus had become repulsive through sin, then how do we apply this to our own lives? At those times when we consider our lives as unholy, does God become a distant figure turning away in disgust; too holy to see us in our real situations? This is central to our view of the character of God. Jesus experienced darkness and isolation from God. If Jesus had not experienced the fullness of this, he could not with full validity and empathy, be able to identify with our fallen state. To experience separation allows Jesus to be our advocate, and what happened in that moment 2,000 years ago remains foundational in our understanding of the character of God.

If God is angry and vengeful then we become surprised at his response to our forefathers who broke relationship:

- Adam and Eve opened the floodgates of evil to our world. Through their rebellion, they really did spoil everything. God's response was simply to engage them in conversation. He walked with them, listened to them, and when they experienced shame and guilt for the first time, and felt awkward with their body image, God provided a sacrifice to meet their need. We do not meet God taking revenge and killing them.

- When Cain killed Abel we do not meet a vengeful God, but we meet God who took up conversation with Cain, seeking to understand. God did not kill Cain. The consequences for Cain were harsh, but we need to remember he'd just murdered his brother [42]. This event records the first murderer (Cain), the first death (Abel), and the first mourners (Adam and Eve), and it records a grieving God who showed his mercy towards Cain.

For several years I've been involved with a charity that runs a disaster-response program. Central to the programs ideology is the question *'where would Jesus be when people are having the worst day of their life'*. If there's a chance he's turned away during our most needy times, we perhaps need to add disclosures to the redemption story; some small-print under Terms and Conditions addressing the excluded areas of coverage.

Revelation introduces us to the symbolism of fire burning in the eyes of God [43] and we can read this and associate this fire with revenge and destruction, or we can find peace in these eyes knowing this fire burns our wickedness, rebellion and sin; destroying anything that will harm us. If we look deeper into these eyes we see tears of pain, tears of joy and tears conjuring up the entire spectrum of emotions experienced by parents as they navigate the maze of loving, protecting and empowering their children whilst giving increased levels of freedom as their children grow and mature.

I consider my family to be very functional and my sons are delights; we have fun and we enjoy each other's company, yet it has taken many years of providing ongoing care and discipleship in a loving environment to reach this point. When the children were young not knowing the difference between right and wrong, we needed to guide them. When they knew this difference and pushed the limits, we'd use a range of sanctions to guide them (usually no screen-time, and early to bed) and this discipline was part and parcel of raising children. My sons now live full lives, they know their identity, and have freedom and security within our family unit.

Many see engagement with Christianity as the giving up of rights and freedom and replacing these with ritual and sacrifice. Yet this notion is inaccurate.

Freedom is not possible without Christ. Even in the most democratic of nations, we do not have complete freedom.

Schizophrenic-God

Of the nine names I've given to veils, this name I admit was the hardest to type. I developed the concept of Schizophrenic-God at the outset of writing this book, but how to include it without causing offence; to those suffering schizophrenia where there is not an easy link between schizophrenia and unstable and violent behaviour; to those with a loved one suffering schizophrenia; and those who become offended through my irreverence. Schizophrenic-God.

I hope you can bear with me on this title.

On the one hand, we can say that God is *'loving and kind'* yet we can hold to the concept that God is also *'mean and vengeful';* representing contradictory demeanours that are incompatible. If God is both loving and mean he becomes irrationally angry and illogically dangerous. He is at odds with himself operating from split personalities, where we become mere subjects living in fear that God may be in a bad mood, with the power to cause serious harm.

ENTITLEMENT-BASED VEILS

Happy-God

Rainbows and unicorns, where God becomes part of the Disney Parade. He's happy and he's all about our happiness. The Law has been fulfilled and grace tastes like doughnuts with God as our personal dentist healing our aching tooth without the need for a needle; we can keep on eating.

Perspective is needed. God is an emotional God, he experiences pain and he experiences joy. God is happy. It's in his nature to be happy; Heaven would be a solemn place if happiness was absent. Yet there are situations that cannot bring happiness to God; there is too much pain and suffering in this world, too many families being torn apart, and too many people needing to flee homes and countries. I remember sitting in a doctor's office after my three-year-old son sustained a serious head injury; this was far from a happy moment for me and Sarah. We felt despair and we felt vulnerable, I consider we were experiencing the heart of God that was broken. Something awful had happened to the one we love. Yet at the same time, we can both speak of God's peace and joy being present.

God is a happy God but the world is not always a happy world, and we need to navigate this dynamic. When we pursue and desire a faith that's all rainbows and unicorns in a constant state of happiness we misunderstand God and wear a veil. It becomes hard to speak of God's love to a hurting world when we interpret God through a veil.

God likes festivals and he's constantly calling us to join him in celebration. God likes laughter and he loves music. These do bring happiness, and God is interested in our happiness, but life in our human frame will never be 100% happy. If we subscribe to a faith that calls for a constant state of happiness we soon become disillusioned the next time we face an inevitable lack of happiness. Happiness dissipates and we feel abandoned, confused and unloved without the tools to persevere.

Genie-God

The genie provides narrative for great story-telling. Genies stem from Arabian folklore and generally depict a spirit imprisoned within a lamp or a bottle. If you release the spirit, usually through a simple process of rubbing the side of the vessel you may get your wishes granted. In effect, a released spirit becomes your personal servant.

It would be a hard task to find a Christian using this terminology (Genie-God) but our actions often mimic the concept. If I pray a certain prayer, God will provide for my needs; if I follow a certain formula – it's like a science – God will answer; if I give to a certain ministry God will reward me. We've entered a transactional cause-and-effect relationship, where we dictate the output by formulating the input. We rub the lamp and out comes blessing.

Safe-God

We desire safety. We desire personal safety and the safety of those around us. It's a natural instinct, and when we do not feel safe we do not feel secure and confident. Safety is a good thing and is something we need to pursue.

In 1943 Abraham Maslow submitted a paper discussing human motivation to Psychological Review [44] entitled "A Theory of Human Motivation". This paper introduced us to 'Maslow's hierarchy of needs'.

In the simplest of terms, Maslow's hierarchy of needs is presented as a pyramid with 5 levels. The bottom two levels represent the most basic of our needs:

1. Physiological needs (the need for food, water, warmth and rest)
2. Safety needs (the need for safety and security)

Once these basic needs are met, Maslow's theory suggests we then have the motivation to seek our psychological needs:

3. Belonging and love needs (the need for friends and intimate relationship)
4. Esteem needs (the need to feel accomplished and the need for prestige)

By meeting our psychological needs we can now seek self-fulfilment, regarded by Maslow as:

5. Self-actualisation needs (the need to reach one's full potential, and the pursuit of creative activities)

Maslow suggests that we need to meet our basic needs (e.g. food and safety) before we can pursue the higher goals of intimacy and fulfilment.

Whilst working in a refugee camp I saw first-hand how this worked. The refugee crisis was dire in need and huge in scope, and thousands of people died before reaching the safety of the refugee camp.

The journey to the camp was dangerous and would last many months, and during this journey, the majority of refugees somehow survived, and somehow found just enough food to eat and enough potable water to drink. Although their most basic needs may have been met, they were not met within a framework of safety. They existed at Level 1 of Maslow's hierarchy of need, and their motivation was fully occupied with the immediate need for personal survival.

After reaching the relative safety of the refugee camp I could observe a change in priorities. Within 24-hours of arriving at the camp, I could sense that the immediate fear of danger had subsided and their motivations now turned to other pressing needs; basic sanitary provisions for their family, a change of clothes, toys for their children and the need to try and connect with people of their same cultural background. Using the safety of the camp as a foundation, the refugees would also look for belonging and even purpose.

After a day or two, several of the refugees would find personal motivation to contribute to the relief effort; to provide translation, to help people with belongings, to carry water, and at times to act as negotiators. In less than 48-hours some refugees had not only achieved a sense of safety, but they also pursued a sense of belonging and betterment, not just for themselves but also for the wider community.

God wants the immediate safety for refugees, and this also becomes a pressing concern for us.

I'm confident that for most of us we have our basic needs met, that we feel safe and we are motivated to improve our lives and see the betterment of society.

Yet, being safe – in the spiritual sense – can mute our ability to take risks and step out in faith, and because of this, spiritual safety can become a barrier to the fullness of life.

If we seek a safe spiritual life, we can start to view God through a veil of safety. We underline verses that talk about Jesus being meek and mild and look to Holy Spirit as the bringer of peace of comfort whilst failing to realise that God's plan's for our lives might not always appear to be the safest option.

God is the provider of ultimate safety, and this safety is within his perfect love and is fully discovered through his plans and purposes for us. The challenge for those seeking spiritual safety, however, is that God is not a tame God and he's usually calling us out of our comfort zone.

Alternatively, we can downplay the seriousness of the sin in our lives and consider that God is only concerned about the big wrongs in this world. Within this situation, we can develop a false sense of safety by using the changing benchmark of societal norms to determine our own level of personal behaviour.

Society doesn't consider gossip, or greed as all that bad these days, and pornography can simply become a personal freedom of choice. Because many societies are becoming more accepting of this general moral tailspin, we can forget that God has not changed and the gap between the benchmark he has called us to and the general state of many societies widens year after year, and for us to take a stand for what we believe, in many instances, requires us to remove our safe-God veil.

God absolutely desires our personal safety, there is no question in this, but our spiritual comfort is different. Just like the picture of the eagle that pushes her young from the safety of her nest, God will shake our spiritual comfort and place of safety, and encourage us to soar to the unchartered territory where life is to be lived to the full.

In reading the above, it remains important that we do not disempower God. God is not a pacifist, and warfare exists in the spiritual realm and we're called to actively engage in this spiritual battle.

Chapter 9
The Tension Between the Day of the Lord and the Love of God

"What a sublime conception is that of a last judgment!" said he,—"a righting of all the wrongs of ages!—a solving of all moral problems, by an unanswerable wisdom! It is, indeed, a wonderful image."

- Harriet Beecher Stowe, *Uncle Tom's Cabin* [45]

A good friend teaches inductive Bible study and often leads students on a journey of discovering Old Testament Kings using long lines of paper complete with key dates and key names. We've often stood around this panoramic view and recounted stories of the more bizarre facts from this period, times where interactions with God seem odd, leaving the only conclusion; there are many mysteries in faith.

The position this book takes is God being present in suffering. He did not cause suffering but he stands with the sufferer, and once invited, he acts on behalf of the sufferer in ways that may not make sense. The closeness of God to suffering can lead to accusations of God being the author of pain, and even when done inadvertently, this oppresses the reputation of God.

God is love, God is Holy, and God upholds justice; justice is needed to remove the root-cause of humanities suffering and oppression.

As a species I consider we have an intuition of future catastrophic events bringing destruction to the earth; be it plague, biological warfare, perhaps structural breakdown leading to global panic and lawlessness. Culture-shapers are aware of this and have tapped into our collective insecurity. Hollywood has plotted the destruction of earth hundreds of times since the 1950s all funded by the public at the box-office; the drama of *Deep Impact,* the action of *2012,* or even the fun of *Ice-Age.* iMDB [46] provides a non-exhaustive list of 283 movies under the category *'End of the World Apocalyptic Disaster Movies'* whilst educational books teach of a catastrophic event wiping out the dinosaurs, and many cults advocate a doomsday narrative. We do seem to have an intuition of future events.

The blame for suffering is at the hands of humanity, or fallen angels, yet it's wrong to adopt a theology of God as a pacifist God. The Bible speaks of the Kingdom of Heaven advancing forcibly through spiritual violence in the spiritual realm.[47] Ephesians[48] informs of this reality and challenges us to enter the spiritual fight. Pure righteousness will destroy pure evil, there will never be an alternative future and God has promised a future void of evil.

One of the most frightening, yet encouraging periods of time recorded in the Bible is the period known as the *'Day of the Lord'*. For believers in Jesus, this is the long-anticipated event ushering in eternal peace. The Book of Revelation details how evil will be destroyed at the hands of God, whilst the Prophet Joel spoke of the *'Day of the Lord',* over 2,500 years ago:

"The day of the Lord is great; it is dreadful. Who can endure it?"[49]

For pursuers of evil, the *'Day of the Lord'* will be catastrophic, yet we have been warned of this coming destruction for several millennia and it's not too late to avoid catastrophe. In many ways God can be seen as two steps ahead – the 2-Step God. He walks ahead of us into the future and provides ample and multiple opportunities for us to turn to him and turn away from evil.

God does not tolerate sin, and this intolerance is one of love's greatest stories where God waits patiently for the disentanglement of people from evil, whilst not infringing on personal choice and freedom, using the full force of patience and mercy for this to happen.

Planet Earth has an expiry date happening at some point in the future, and this is both certain and inescapable; to quote one of my lecturers, *"no one will be able to call-in-sick that day"*. The challenge of modern living, for many cultures, is the silencing of the spiritual narrative, and replacing this narrative with the pursuit of temporal pleasure and promotion.

Two thousand years ago Paul wrote to his companion Timothy warning about the signs of the end of the age:

"Don't be naive. There are difficult times ahead. As the end approaches, people are going to be self-absorbed, money-hungry, self-promoting, stuck-up, profane, contemptuous of parents, crude, coarse, dog-eat-dog, unbending, slanderers, impulsively wild, savage, cynical, treacherous, ruthless, bloated windbags, addicted to lust, and allergic to God".[50]

Unfortunately, it doesn't take long to see many of these vices demonstrated in society today.

Nature displays the wonders of God, and our conscience is a spiritual provision to help find God. We have an inbuilt desire for justice, and our senses perceive the reality of God. Even pain can alert us to the need for a healer, and our souls yearn to belong, to be loved and to discover purpose. We were never left alone, and we have never been without the ability to find God. In its written form, the Bible remains the World's bestselling book with over 5-billion copies produced in global languages.[51]

God became human to live amongst us, and the Spirit is given to continue this demonstration of God's love. Preceding the '*Day of the Lord*'[52] we have '*Days of the Spirit*'[53] where spiritual gifts intensify through the nations, and through the generations as demonstrations of God's love and care for people:

"'In the last days, God says, I will pour out my Spirit on all people. Your sons and daughters will prophesy, your young men will see visions, your old men will dream dreams. Even on my servants, both men and women, I will pour out my Spirit in those days, and they will prophesy. I will show wonders in the heavens above and signs on the earth below, blood and fire and billows of smoke. The sun will be turned to darkness

and the moon to blood before the coming of the great and glorious day of the Lord. And everyone who calls on the name of the Lord will be saved." [54]

A solitary star pronounced the first coming of Jesus. The second coming of Jesus and the end of our age will be announced through the most remarkable and astounding cosmic wonders that no one will be able to miss:

"I will show wonders in the heavens above and signs on the earth below, blood and fire and billows of smoke. The sun will be turned to darkness and the moon to blood before the coming of the great and glorious day of the Lord." [55]

True to the character of God we discover mercy in these unfolding events. Perhaps the most famous imagery from this period is the *'Four Horsemen of the Apocalypse'* [56] where each rider journeys to earth following the breaking of a seal. There appear to be gaps, interludes, between the release of the Horsemen; the White Horse preceding the Red Horse, preceding the Black Horse, preceding the Pale Horse; conquest leading to war, leading to famine and ultimately leading to death; interludes for people to respond to God. This is in alignment with what we know of God; he is compassionate and slow to anger. God, however, will not tolerate sin for eternity. The Holy God has to deal with the horror of evil, but God always has mercy on those who seek him.

The *Day of the Lord* isn't the one flaw in God's exemplary character, nor does it flow in opposite direction to the logic and flow of this book. Yet, there can remain a tension between the *Day of the Lord* and the unconditional and un-surpassing love of Jesus, but with the right understanding and knowledge that evil cannot exist eternally in the same sphere as God-believers, we can move on with confidence.

God is certainly not a pacifist-God, and evil will be dealt with through violence. This is the love of God.

The first coming of Jesus was not widely known as he was born into relative obscurity. The second coming of Jesus will be a global event. The man Jesus came with character and left his Godly nature behind. The second coming of Jesus will display the fullness of his nature. Jesus as full man did not come to judge, yet triumphant Christ the King of the second coming will judge. Jesus as full man was tempted like no other, yet he resisted the temptation to call upon legions of Angels. The second coming of Jesus will see Jesus in full glory flanked by the massed ranks of the nation of warrior angels.

The Bible contains the story of man. And herein lies the challenge. It records our history, our beginnings and our endings. It tells stories of courage, hope, and faith, whilst not covering over humanity's tendency towards ridiculous stupidity. Not every story in the Bible is condoned by God; many stories are there to guide us through spiritual mystery, whilst many stories recount periods where God had been forgotten. *"Meaningless! Meaningless! ... everything is Meaningless"* [57] is a famous quote from the Bible; yet it does not represent God, but it does represent a God who is comfortable with our questioning. Laid bare, the Bible is an epic romance, with relationship and redemption being the narrative. The Bible can remain mysterious, yet there is a clear message. God makes his intentions known and provides us with all we need to follow.

The Bible has been the source of faith, reflection, debate and anger for generations. It's inspired art, customs, literature and war. It can be the source of hope and it can be the source of anger. How can this be?

In the children's classic, Goodnight Mister Tom,[58] Magorian introduces us to young Willie; a shy, nervous boy who along with thousands of other children is evacuated from London as Britain edges ever closer to war. Through the evacuation, Willie comes under the care of Mister Tom, a kindly and ageing reclusive widow who'd lost his own son shortly after birth.

As the book develops, Tom learns of the tragic circumstances leading to Willie being so guarded. As Tom and Willie's relationship develops, a history of abuse and punishment at the hands of Willie's mother comes to light. Willie's mother is introduced as a dangerous religious woman using

God and the Bible as justification to beat the sin out of young Willie. Like many abuse victims, Willie had taken on a victim mentality and the identity of a bad person with punishment being the direct result of his actions. Willie brought abuse upon himself because he deserved it and his perspective on God was fear-based:

> *"Mum said war was a punishment from God for people's sins, so he'd better watch out. She didn't tell him what to watch out for, though."* [59]

This was Willie's dilemma. Willie wrongly believed he and nations were punished by God because they were sinners; the confusion faced by Willie, however, was to know what behaviour was worthy of a beating. Willie's mother considered her son full of sin and acted on behalf of God by physically and emotionally abusing Willie; deeming this her righteous duty.

It's through the gentleness of Mister Tom that Willie learns this not to be true.

When we have the wrong impression of God we can start to believe God punishes those he loves; through calamity, the onset of disease, or God using someone to do the beating on his behalf.

For millions of believers, the Bible is our source of faith, wisdom, and inspiration. It becomes our living spiritual guide when navigating the moral, political, and social dynamics of society. Yet, if taken out of context the Bible can fuel negativity. It can seem contradictory, aggressive, and cause people to lose track of reality.

There is danger in reading the Bible from an abstract perspective. Later in this book we'll look at the decision by God to not hide unsavoury members of his family tree; he tells their stories. He does not shy away from family drama, and he did not photo-shop the Old Testament; the good, the bad and the down-right terrible are on display. When looking through the lives of some Biblical characters, and some Biblical events we can develop wrong impressions of God.

King David, commended by God, and a man after God's own heart, whose family line Jesus would be born into committed one of the most cowardly acts in the Bible. King David had sex with the wife of one of his most loyal and dedicated warriors, who at the time of David's moment of pleasure, was on the battle-field courageously fighting for David. The story did not end well for Uriah.

Moments after the bliss of coitus had evaporated; all that was left was the bitter after-taste. David realised his mistake and needed a cover-up. He'd eaten bitter forbidden fruit and was left tormented. David recalled Uriah from the battle-front, arranged for Uriah to get drunk and then suggested Uriah goes home to be with his wife. Without DNA testing there would be no question as to who the father was; the timing would fit perfectly with Uriah's unexpected home-leave. However, David had not considered the strength of Uriah's character, his allegiance to David's throne, and the nation of Israel:

"Uriah was unwilling to violate the ancient kingdom rule applying to warriors in active service. Rather than go home to his own bed, he preferred to remain with the palace troops." [60]

Time ticked on, and David became increasingly incensed; ultimately leading to David's betrayal. David deployed Uriah to the front line and issued a command that when the fighting is the fiercest, for the army to retreat leaving Uriah outnumbered and cut-off. This command was followed.

Uriah became cut-off and true to his character I have no doubt Uriah fought to the bitter end with devotion to King and country providing the last drop of adrenaline and strength. I'm sure Uriah was not alone; I imagine loyal warriors would not leave Uriah as they continued their doomed mission. Isolated with no retreat, moment by moment, death by death these hardy warriors would fall. *'For King and country'* may have been their final call as they took one last but futile heroic stand; fallen sons on a distant and cruel battlefield. They died for king and country not knowing their king had plotted their downfall.

Yet, God loved David and we may conclude that God turned a blind eye to David's abuse of position to satisfy his sexual cravings, and destroy any obstacles.

One of the lowest parts of this dismal story sees King David dispatch Uriah to the front line carrying the Royal Command ordering the battlefield tactics. In effect, Uriah carried his own death-sentence to the front-line.

David abused his authority; he betrayed, murdered and lied.

Earlier we looked at the simple equation; God is good and the devil is bad. When bad things happen we know which side of the equation has determined the answer. David acted under the influence of the fallen kingdom and these events resulted in death, yet God cancelled the power of death over David's life.

The sequence of events did not end well for Uriah, but nor did they end well for King David. David lost a great deal and would never be the same again. He was inflicted with personal calamity and loss. God was angry with David, and David felt God's discipline. Yet, God loved David and David loved God. Forgiveness of wickedness, rebellion and sin was measured out to David and their love relationship restored.

Uriah was highly commended in the book of Hebrews as a man of great courage and honour, and Bathsheba was honoured and grafted into the lineage of Jesus [61]. A bad situation was not over-looked but was redeemed. Lust, betrayal and murder had happened and discipline was engaged.

David became a broken man and opened his life for the world to see. We catch a glimpse of this immense inner struggle David continued to experience through the remainder of his life:

"Have mercy on me, O God, according to your steadfast love; according to your abundant mercy blot out my transgressions. Wash me thoroughly from my iniquity, and cleanse me from my sin!" [62]

David repented, was broken, and experienced the anger of God, and his life became marked by episodes of personal tragedy. He'd plotted evil and hurt two people whom God dearly loved. God's love is jealous and God's love became angered. Yet, God's forgiveness flowed like a river back to the soul of David.

David subjected himself to the fallen kingdom where for a period of time he exhibited these values in the physical.

Chapter 10
A Return to Innocence

"Parents can only give good advice or put them on the right paths, but the final forming of a person's character lies in their own hands."

- Anne Frank [63]

In the physical, it's not possible to return to Eden, yet in the spiritual, the completed works of Jesus transforms us as though we had never sinned; the perfect factory reset button. Kurt Vonnegut, in his acclaimed anti-war novel 'Slaughter-House Five' provides an at times dark account of the stories of Billy Pilgrim; an American soldier enlisted as a chaplain's assistant. Billy is poorly trained, ill-equipped, subjected to episodes of time-travel and has no stomach for war; consequently, Billy refuses to fight and is taken captive in 1944 during the Battle of the Bulge. Vonnegut takes the reader through the fire-bombing of a German city, an image that has captivated my mind of a return to a time before war, or war in reverse, a return to innocence.

"American planes, full of holes and wounded men and corpses, took off backwards from an airfield in England. Over France, a few German fighter planes flew at them backwards, sucked bullets and shell fragments from some of the planes and crewmen.

The formation flew backwards over a German city that was in flames. The bombers opened their bomb bay doors, exerted a miraculous magnetism which shrunk the fires, gathered them into cylindrical steel containers, and lifted the containers into the bellies of the planes. The Germans below had miraculous devices of their own, which were long steel tubes. They used them to suck more fragments from the crewmen and planes ... over France ... German fighters came up again, made everything and everybody as good as new.

When the bombers got back to their base, the steel cylinders were taken from the racks and shipped back to the United States of America, where factories were operating night and day, dismantling the cylinders, separating the dangerous contents into minerals ... The minerals were then shipped to specialists in remote areas. It was their business to put them into the ground, to hide them cleverly, so they would never hurt anybody ever again.

The American fliers turned in their uniforms, became high school kids. And Hitler turned into a baby ... everybody turned into a baby, and all humanity, without exception, conspired biologically to produce two perfect people named Adam and Eve".[64]

Chapter 11
Shadowlands

"Beware lest you lose the substance by grasping at the shadow."

- Aesop, *The Dog and the Shadow* [65]

The devil deploys tactics to keep us from attaining full confidence in our identity. We're made in the spiritual image of God and our true identity comes from God. The devil will try and taint God's reputation, and mess with our identity through undermining God, telling lies, twisting the truth, causing confusion and speaking accusation. It really is a war for hearts and minds, and military leaders understand this dynamic through the power of psychological warfare:

"Various techniques are used, and are aimed at influencing a target audience's value system, belief system, emotions, motives, reasoning, or behavior. It is used to induce confessions or reinforce attitudes and behaviors favorable to the originator's objectives." [66]

Genghis Khan became notorious for adopting similar tactics of provoking mass terror to defeat the will of the enemy.

With the intention of the Dark-Kingdom being to kill, steal and destroy it's no wonder so many people struggle with identity, self-image and self-worth. We fall foul of the devil's propaganda machine.

Social-commentators refer to our current generation as *Generation-Like* or the *selfie-generation*. In April 2016 The Daily Mail [67] reported how we share 880 billion selfies on social media each year, and researchers are making increasing connection between posting a selfie and the need for social validation and approval gained through the numbers of *likes* achieved.

As a parent, I'm encouraged that our school facilitates workshops on cyber-safety and how to navigate social media. The school facilitates these sessions through concern at the growing numbers of pre-teens needing validation on their physical appearance. A report shared at one of these sessions highlighted research linking the amount of flesh revealed in a *selfie* and the number of *likes* generated. I commend the school for tackling this issue by helping define true beauty; to work alongside researchers and provide resources, but the challenge of self-image and identity faced by children and teenagers today is significant and appears relentless.

The country that's adopted my family is affectionately known as the 'lucky country', and we do feel blessed to call Australia home. Yet, our lucky country has an alarming problem of teen suicide, self-harm and addictions. The number two cause of death for Australian young people is suicide; second only to motor vehicle accidents. Melbourne's respected Royal Children's Hospital reports *"suicide rates among 15-24 year old males have trebled between 1960 and 1990."* [68]

I doubt we need more evidence of the struggle for identity, and it's important we meet Jesus without a veil. 2,000 years ago Paul spoke of this reality

"But whenever anyone turns to the Lord, the veil is taken away." [69]

Chapter 12
Dealing with a Polytheistic Mindset

"Idolatry, then, is always polytheism, an aimless passing from one lord to another. Idolatry does not offer a journey but rather a plethora of paths leading nowhere and forming a vast labyrinth."

– Pope Francis [70]

As Christians, we can hold confidently to the notion of one true God. This is monotheism, and we become perplexed when trying to comprehend polytheistic faiths. Yet, how many times do we believe in one true God, yet subconsciously at least, consider he has split personalities.

That somehow, the God who never changes actually did change between the Old and New Testaments. Where God might be angry one day and happy the next; he's either blessing or he's cursing, either healing or destroying. Leaving us in a position where we're never fully confident which personality we're going to get. To the extreme, this might be considered a Schizophrenic God, and we've become followers of a polytheistic religion. Although these might be considered extreme polar ends of a God continuum, many do carry a niggling question or concern that finds alignment along the continuum of these extremes.

Many consider ourselves God-believers; but deep down, in the quietness of our hearts, and confusion of our minds, we'd consider we do believe in a monotheistic God but through the filter of a polytheistic mindset.

Chapter 13
Being Free of Polytheistic thinking

"Guide my eyes so I can see."

– Joseph Matthews [72]

At first appearance, it's rather odd, a poor choice from a loving God to place innocence next to evil; allowing for their coexistence, and to not expect a bad outcome. After all, God had the entire universe to expel evil. Adam and Eve knew of evil but had not experienced it; similar to the animal kingdom where a newborn senses danger from a prowling predator but until the first attack, it remains a concept only. Adam and Eve would have an awareness of evil; however, evil still remained an alien concept to them.

Upon arriving in Narnia; Digory, Polly, Uncle Andrew, and the Cabby with his four-legged companion 'Strawberry' become immersed in the presence of Aslan and captivated whilst witnessing the creation song. Upon declaring "Narnia is established" Aslan continues:

"For though the world is not five hours old an evil has already entered it." 'Evil' was a word the gathered creatures were not familiar with and the conversation ensued with great mystery ... "What did he say had entered the world? -A Neevil – What's a Neevil? – No, he didn't say a Neevil, he said a weevil – Well, what's that?" [73]

The question of the origin of evil finds not an easy answer, remaining in the context of mystery. Despite its mystery, the challenge of evil had now become our challenge; a challenge Jesus also had to overcome.

When we're challenged in our understanding of God, and start to view the Bible through a lens of uncertainty and insecurity, we struggle to comprehend apparent inconsistencies found in the Bible. And when the

Bible becomes a tool in dislodging our security, we desperately need to turn to God and seek meaning. The following passages appear at polar ends to each other and form a backdrop to the continuing discussion of this book:

"God saw all that he had made, and it was very good." [74]

And,

"However, in the cities of the nations the Lord your God is giving you as an inheritance, do not leave alive anything that breathes. Completely destroy them." [75]

God created humanity and said 'we are very good.'[76] Several books later God gives the order to conquer Canaan and kill every man, woman and child. This raises many questions.

When reading the Bible without a good understanding of the character of God, and are confronted with challenging circumstances, we can easily lose confidence in the God we'd grown accustomed to or the God we'd hoped to be loving and kind.

The motivation of God is to *'bring life and have it to the full,'*[77] while the motivation of the devil is to *'steal and kill and destroy.'*[78] When we see destruction in the Bible or destruction in the 21st Century, we need to ask *'who's to blame?'*

Many Christians have difficulties explaining God in the Old Testament, whilst many sceptics use the Old Testament as proof that God is a God of war, a harsh judge, and is tyrannical. God has never been to war and war breaks his heart as it destroys the relationship with his people. It's almost as though God gets a lot of credit for the schemes of the devil, and the actions of humans.

We need to address the hurdles standing in the way of our identity, whilst discussing the wrong opinions we form giving God a poor reputation. Many hurdles come through wearing the veils that defray

God's character. Previously, we identified nine of these veils based on **Fear**, **Doubt** and **Entitlement**.

As a father, I recently reached the dreaded day where my growing son exclaimed 'you're far too protective dad'. Thankfully, for this time at least, it was more an observation rather than an attack on my identity. Yet it did strike me. Am I too protective? Isn't it my role as a father to be protective? But over-protective, really? I considered the consequences if I remained over-protective, and realised how my desire for good has the potential to cause a barrier. I wonder if this might be the same with God. God desires the best for us, yet to achieve this we need to walk together in a position of free-will:

> *"Astonishingly, the Creator seldom imposes himself on his creatures ... when lesser gods attract, God withdraws, honouring our fatal freedom to ignore him."* [79]

God understands this dynamic. He's accused of being tyrannical; yet, it's perhaps closer to reality if we accuse God of being too submissive to our own desires. Anais Nin captures this concept beautifully:

> *"And the day came when the risk to remain tight in a bud was more painful than the risk it took to blossom."* [80]

If my children aren't able to develop from absolute dependency on me as their father, I'd have failed in my calling as a father; we now discover together, grow together and discuss together. Sharing each other's company becomes a choice, and is a delight and pleasure. My deepest desire now is that love will grow between me and my sons out of choice, not obligation. A manipulated person will never fully understand free will and the choice to love.

As a species, we continue to let veils cover our face, and we continue to live with a tainted image of the beauty of God, allowing veils to produce a skewed image of God. God has come to bring life and 'life to the full' [81] and this is a promise, and it's a wonderful promise. God really does desire for you and for me to become the best version of us that we can be. His dreams, His plans and His desires for us are beyond comprehension, they are unfathomably beautiful. If we're not careful our veils can get in the way, robbing our inheritance, whilst breaking down our identity. A father instils identity to a child, and our true identity comes from God. If this transfer of identity from God to child is filtered through a veil our identity becomes distorted.

These veils are often formed subtly. We don't necessarily choose them, and we may not be aware when we're wearing them. Many times these veils are worn through inadvertently allowing the values of the kingdom of darkness to be intertwined with our narratives. The devil operates in the shadows, and rarely carries out direct accusations; rather, he challenges our security and shakes our confidence. He sows seeds of doubt, we water them, and he watches them grow.

Nitrogen narcosis is a strange predicament caused by diving at depth. It creeps up on unsuspecting victims and influences the body through increasing amounts of danger, leaving the host ignorant to the dangerous changes they are going through.

Numbers of years ago I experienced nitrogen narcosis during an advanced diving course, with part of the course designed to expose divers to the impact of narcosis. The dive was planned shore-side with our instructor detailing various tests and activities to be carried out at a depth where narcosis would have an impact.

I didn't excel at high-school maths; nonetheless, I considered giving answers to the most rudimentary of maths questions – even under the influence of narcosis – a simple activity. Another test required the construction of a square consisting of four straight pieces of Meccano style plastic and four interlocking corner pieces, contained within a pouch. A simple square. We practised on the surface and a perfect square was formed in less than 30 seconds.

The dive commenced and after reaching the required depth my buddy and I were given a slate to answer simple maths questions: $2 + 2$, $5 - 3$. These were easy questions fit for a primary school classroom rather than an advanced course for adults. Needless to say, I wrote my answers with little need for thought. The answers seemed to roll readily from my fingers to the slate. The second activity was harder, not so much the construction side of the activity, rather the challenge of accessing the equipment through a closed pouch. Yet even at depths, untying the knot was a relatively straightforward experience, and despite having to retain the plastic objects from floating away, the exercise was still completed in less than a few minutes.

I was satisfied with my efforts and within a few short minutes, our instructor made the necessary hand-signals beginning our planned ascent, complete with decompression stops. We reached shore-side, doffed our equipment and waited for debriefing.

I had confidence in my underwater abilities of basic construction and childhood mathematics. On the surface $2 + 2 = 4$, at depth and under the influence of narcosis $2 + 2$ became a long and random string of numbers, dotted with punctuation and the odd letter. My perfect square now resembled the first two rungs of a ladder. How could I have been so wrong? The answer is narcosis.

In its Greek form, *narke*; narcosis is described as a *"temporary decline or loss of senses and movement, numbness."*[82] A more colloquial definition would simply say I was 'high' where I'd experienced the anaesthetic effects of high-pressure gases mirroring the use of narcotics. I'd willingly paid good money to experience this, to enter a dangerous environment where the laws of physics were enjoying a field-day, hijacking my judgement and rendering me useless even in the simplest of activities, whilst removing my ability to make any worthwhile decision besides the reckless ones. I'd truly mastered the art of foolishness and attained a feat I've rarely experienced: overconfidence.

With nitrogen narcosis the deeper you descend the deeper the experience. I remember reading an account of an unfortunate diver, who thankfully lived to tell the tale; the deeper he dived, the funnier it became to remove his breathing apparatus and swallow water. The more water he swallowed the funnier it became and he'd entered a frightening spiral of demise. He was experiencing the cruel reality of losing control of his mental abilities, and laughing all the way. There really is a good reason why divers use the buddy-system and rigorously plan dives shore-side.

A diver can learn the effects of narcosis, learn how to avoid it, but it still remains impossible to develop any type of tolerance. By plunging deeper into danger the grip of narcosis slowly wraps its tentacles around the victim's mind resulting in damage to the body. The good news, in fact, it's great news, is the effects of narcosis are as temporary as the length remained at the depth. It's fully reversible and there's no reported long-term impact. It's almost as though the narcosis was never there.

The veils we wear are similar in nature to the impact of narcosis. They remain hidden, and we may not be aware when we're wearing them. One of the first observable signs of narcosis is impeded vision; likewise, veils impact our vision and provide an unwanted filter. Whilst experiencing narcosis, I would have bet my bottom dollar that my square was a square – I had no doubt it was a square. I could see it, I could feel it, I had complete confidence it was a square, I'd even constructed it. Yet I was thoroughly mistaken in my opinion.

During times in my life where I've worn a veil, I've remained ignorant that my view of God was impaired and I could no longer see the beauty of God in full clarity. I'd formed an opinion of God and I was growing surer of my wrong conclusion; I had clouded my view with a veil.

In my diving experience, I needed an instructor and a buddy to help me navigate away from the narcosis. In my spiritual life, I need an instructor and a buddy. God sent the spirit to remove the veil and a spiritual community to help me should I fall too deep, or help me to realise that I'm interpreting God and life through a veil.

When my narrative starts using values and words contrary to the narrative of the Kingdom of God then similar to narcosis, it's a sign I'm wearing a veil. Words, values and actions similar to; hostility, hate, taking or giving offence, destruction, obscurity, isolation, taking on or giving accusation, and experiencing a sense of worthlessness, self-doubt and self-pity are the danger signs that I'm diving too deep. Unless I start my ascent, I can become like the diver who had entered a dangerous spiral of removing his air supply and drinking the water that would ultimately defeat him.

When we view God through the veils, God will most likely remain shrouded in the mystery that we are called to fathom. When we develop theory and theology grounded on mystery, we can start to present a God who can be distant and vague, mean and vengeful, rather than loving and kind.

Nitrogen Narcosis is a fitting analogy of the veils that we wear.

Chapter 14
Segue Jesus

"An uninterrupted transition"

– Segue, dictionary.com [83]

For many years I've pondered the differences between the Old Testament and the New Testament, the differences between Law and Grace, and the role of God in both. At a recent prayer time, we were singing *"There is none like you"* [84] a song penned in the presence of God blessing worshippers the world over; truly, a God-inspired song. The song contains beautiful imagery of the safety of children in the arms of a loving God. Several minutes earlier my morning routine had been rocked, I joined the collective world in shock with the abduction of 200 Nigerian schoolgirls at the hands of Boko Haram. I lost the motivation to sing, my mind was full of questions as I wrestled with this concept of children being safe in the arms of God and the real world of Boko Haram.

How could a loving God allow this to happen? My mind turned to the actions of God in the Old Testament and the teachings of Jesus in the New Testament, and for a short while the two were not making sense; they no longer appeared compatible. The gulf that existed between the Conquest of Canaan and the love of Jesus was forming a vast dichotomy.

I once visualised a scene in heaven, a conversation amongst the God-head just prior to Jesus entering earth.

The God-head are executives of a dominant global corporation, yet times were changing, and it was becoming apparent they could no longer silence or ignore those who didn't like their services. They could no longer hire thugs to open up new markets and deal with competitors. As executives, they were distant, male and not willing to change; unable to change and inept to act.

They did, reluctantly, however, acknowledge these changing times, and realised they needed to engage the community and win back trust with the customer-base. They hired a Public Relations firm.

The Public Relations firm assessed the situation and developed strategy. The executives were told to loosen their ties a little, roll up their sleeves, and get a little dirt on their expensive polished leather shoes. To come down from their ivory tower and take a road trip.

Lessons were given on how to look sincere, how to hold a baby for that perfect photo-opportunity, and how to deal with anger at public meetings. Jesus was selected for this road-trip and press-releases were meticulously written. As this strategy rolled out, Jesus became the human face of the distant mystery, a corporate make-over was given and hopefully, all would be well.

Comical maybe; correct, it couldn't be further, and although my picture misrepresents God, I'd imagine it does find traction with many concerns people harbour about God being tyrannical, harsh, and quick to smite.

It's hard to fully comprehend all that Jesus did for us; all he took on for us. The depths of pain and sorrow and the agony of suffering he endured are beyond our ability to grasp. In Jesus, God made himself nothing, allowing himself to be trampled by humanity. He voluntarily experienced every emotion, every fear, every doubt, every temptation, and every humiliation common to humanity.

He voluntarily experienced this because of His absolute love for us. He held nothing back, restraining the temptation to use his nature and instead exhibited his life through character, modelling voluntary love and sacrifice.

Jesus was the exact representation of God, and unlike my parody, the entrance of Jesus to the human environment was not a public relations tour, but the perfect segue. The perfect continuation of what Edwards refers to as *"The Divine Romance"*[85] between God and his creation. Jesus revealed the mystery of God in fullness.

The paradox of God is that he can remain a mystery yet also personable. On the mystery side God is spirit (beyond matter, time and space); uncreated, encompassing infinite attributes; infinite in presence, infinite in knowledge, and infinite in power. On the personable side, we see God as loving, kind, gracious and compassionate, with a tender emotional heart and He's not ashamed to exhibit these emotions. God, in walking with us, exposes himself to the same emotions that we experience.

The Bible records God as being able to think, to feel, and to choose. God grieved and experienced sorrow;[86] he's suffered a broken heart;[87] he's wept[88] and groaned at situations;[89] he's angered,[90] and takes delight.[91] God sings,[92] ponders,[93] and even whistles.[94] While at appropriate times, he's displeased with our actions.[95] God also changes his mind to incorporate our actions, our thinking, and our intentions.[96] The Bible shows God withholding judgment, whilst extending grace and mercy in the hope we turn to God.

Chapter 15
Why people Suffer

"Even pain can alert us to the need for a healer."

– Nicholas Matthews [97]

The first of our species; Adam and Eve had a fall, and we inherited their lameness. God had no intention for us to suffer, and our human bodies were not designed for pain. The question as to the origin of evil is a mystery, yet the very existence of evil is described by Pope Paul VI as: *"a terrible reality, mysterious and frightening."*[98] Evil is often referred to as a void, yet it's more than an absence it's a sinister reality. In November 1972 Pope Paul VI delivered a speech *"Confronting the Devil's Power"*[99] addressing evil in terrifying terms:

"Evil is not merely an absence of something but an active force, a living, spiritual being that is perverted and that perverts others"[100]

People suffer because of evil. Why is evil tolerated? Where does evil come from? These are amongst the biggest questions of them all.

Evil advocates our turning from God and allows sin to enter. There will always be a consequence for sin, and Paul provides the following understanding:

"the wages of sin is death, but the gift of God is eternal life."[101]

Sin requires death; yours, mine or the death of a kinsman-redeemer. Through the Old Testament the death of an animal was sufficient, and in the New Testament the death of a human was required. We needed a second Adam to be our kinsman redeemer. The man Jesus fulfilled this role – as our second Adam – and purchased our freedom from the slave market of death.

The question of *'why people suffer'* needs to be seen in the context of our turning from God and adopting the principles of the world, and following a value system non-aligned to God's character. At worst, some of our current and historical governing systems follow values under control of the devil. When we choose to reside in this worlds' value system we distance our identity from God and live contrary to how our body, soul and spirit were designed to exist.

The first of our species did have a fall, we inherited this lameness, but Jesus paid the required price to redeem us.

Chapter 16
The Suffering God

"There is a LIGHT in this world. A healing spirit more powerful than any darkness we may encounter."

– Richard Attenborough [102]

God, through Jesus, suffered the complete sum total of humanities generational pain and suffering from beginning to end by taking it upon himself at the cross. When we encounter pain and suffering in the Bible we sympathise with God as he suffered this.

When Jericho was routed, God would physically suffer their pain to the point of death. When we read how Cain killed Abel, when we hear news of the horrendous conditions of captivity, and we hear the pain of a mother losing her only child, perhaps instead of blaming God we need to focus on the love of God. Jericho's pain, the entire pain of humanity was collected, packaged and injected into God as he suffered the cross.

God knows the human frame well, he's lived inside one, and he's shared the entire plethora of human emotion. There is a marked difference between a Travel Agent and a Travel Guide. A good agent will know their information; they will research well, they'll ask the right questions, and study relevant resources giving the best service to their clientele. They can anticipate needs and advice accordingly. Yet, they may have never travelled to the places or experienced the cultures in which they are selling; they remain academically informed but experientially lacking.

A travel guide is different. They are on the ground, leading through experience.

God became our Travel Guide.

"The servant grew up before God—a scrawny seedling, a scrubby plant in a parched field. There was nothing attractive about him, nothing to cause us to take a second look. He was looked down on and passed over, a man who suffered, who knew pain firsthand. One look at him and people turned away. We looked down on him, thought he was scum. But the fact is, it was our pains he carried—our disfigurements, all the things wrong with us. We thought he brought it on himself, that God was punishing him for his own failures. But it was our sins that did that to him, that ripped and tore and crushed him—our sins! He took the punishment, and that made us whole. Through his bruises we get healed. We're all like sheep who've wandered off and gotten lost. We've all done our own thing, gone our own way. And God has piled all our sins, everything we've done wrong, on him, on him". [103]

The poetical beauty of Isaiah, as captured by Peterson, gives a sobering account of the brokenness of God. Only when we stop and digest the depths of this passage do we begin to fathom Jesus in his fullness. Isaiah provides an overview of the universal assault and humiliation on God, and the plan of annihilation and destruction of Jesus. God suffers alongside us. He really was crushed for our iniquities.

If Jesus had written an autobiography, with a focus on overcoming adversity, it may have read similar to this:

I have a kingdom, and I've lived the life of Royalty, but I gave all this up. I left behind my robes, my glory, and my warriors, and upon entering earth I became an enemy of the state.

I was born under military occupation, born a Jew. The system sought to take my life, and I survived attempted infanticide. A King was bent on my destruction, this King, King Herod, commonly referred to as the 'madman'[104] and 'evil genius of the Judean nation,'[105] regarded me as a threat.

When I was young my parents had to flee our hometown and we soon became an internally-displaced family; later becoming refugees. My early life was a life-on-the-run. What's now known as the 'Murder of the Innocents'[106] took place in my hometown; a micro-genocide. The children of my town were destroyed in the hope that I'd be one of them. A town's children killed because of hatred towards me. I was too young to comprehend any of this, and I needed mum and dad to save me. Many children died in the effort to kill me.

As time went on, mum and dad returned home; yet danger was never far away. Herod's son succeeded in killing my cousin, and his grandson later killed many close friends and persecuted those who stood with me.

Without any doubt, I was an enemy of the state.

It wasn't easy for mum, with confusion surrounding her pregnancy, and the social customs of the day made this hard. If dad had not understood he could've had mum murdered through Deuterocanonical tradition[107] because of her pregnancy being pre-marriage; an act killing us both.

Looking back, mum had it hard. The Romans wanted to count us, see how many of us there were. To do this they made people go back to their hometown rather than allow them to be counted where they were living. The problem for mum and dad is that mum was heavily pregnant by this stage and the journey was hard.

I mentioned the *'Murder of the Innocents,'* well this was in mum's hometown, a small town where people knew each other. The stress for mum to hear the stories of her friends losing their own children in such a cruel way was hard for her. Mum was young and poor and could only afford turtle-doves as a sacrifice, but mum was strong and she overcame hardships. She persevered through many tribulations.

Suffering was close at hand for our family, and my early years were not easy, but nor were my mum's, and in many ways, it had only begun. No mother should watch her son be tortured.

I had a lot to learn, and I endured much. Yet, this allowed me to understand the human spirit, and the human condition. The world can be a cruel place, and cruelty was never far from me. I was never a criminal, but I was killed as a criminal. I was never a slave, but I was sold for cash. I was never a child-soldier, but I fled soldiers as a child.

Being fully human my body was pushed to the limits and I experienced every physical pain and discomfort. I've been hungry, and I've been thirsty. I've been humiliated through nakedness, and I've known torture. Yet despite the physical abuse, sometimes the emotional stress and anxiety were harder and I've known loneliness to the point of despair, and at times sleep deprivation has taken its hold on me. Temptation was a reality for me, and it seems it was never far away as I experienced every type of temptation.

It wasn't all tough, though, there were times of celebration, times where I could get away with my mates and it was just us.

Looking back on my years on earth, Isaiah was right. I had much to learn and I needed to grow. I thank mum and dad, and it gets me emotional when I look back at all they went through. I grew-up in the human frame and I now know this human frame well.

The reason people wanted me killed was because of my purpose. I was the chosen one, the one my people had been waiting for, for hundreds of years. I came to lead people to glory and their eternal home, to put right their relationship with Father. I did not come with pomp and ceremony, nor did I use the full resources of my kingdom to support me.

I was a leader, but I walked a humble path. I was resolute in my determination, yet I disappointed many who were looking for a hero and a military leader. Some believed I misrepresented their cause. It seemed the older I got more people became angry with me, I couldn't even go back home without it being awkward.

The pressure to conform and lead differently was immense. I've known failure first-hand. One of my team became a thief and stole money from us. It's hard to lose a friend, even when they valued my life less than a handful of silver coins. There were six attempts on my life causing me trauma and pain, but Judas' attempt was the hardest to take.

I began my public ministry when I was about 30, and it seems I'd been preparing for this my whole life. After being baptised I spent 40-days in the wilderness fasting and praying. I'm sure you can imagine how physically and emotionally vulnerable I'd become. This wasn't just a personal struggle, though; my adversary the devil turned up and threw temptation after temptation my way.

Shortly after my time in the wilderness, I found myself in the hustle and bustle of the synagogue. I was reading from Isaiah when the crowd turned. Reflecting on this time, Luke wrote: *"all in the synagogue were filled with wrath."*[108] This wrath saw me man-handled and thrust down to the floor by the hands of a violent mob, for sure, they wanted my blood. They moved with one intention to toss me headlong from the top of the hill, if they'd been successful, they'd have achieved more than my adversary in the desert.

Growing up, I learned the plans my father had for me, studying the prophets and the poetry of the Old Testament I started to piece together the dreadful fate that was mine, yet not this day. My time was to come.

By now I was in the third year of public ministry, and in the Temple at Jerusalem. My words had been taken as blasphemy, a crime carrying the death sentence by stoning. Unlike the Synagogue-mob, this mob didn't even look to take me off the sacred ground and were intent on stoning me in the place my words fell. Their attempts failed and had become the fourth recorded attempt on my life. The angry mob tried again but I averted arrest and stoning.

I knew this couldn't keep going, though. Either I had to run, or change my message. No way. The Temple was the place I'd come to find closeness with Father but with all the noise and hatred it wasn't easy.

As the months passed, I enjoyed family and friends, and the festivals, but I knew my fate. I was well versed in the prophets, and I knew who I was. What I was to do, and where I was going. I mentioned how there were six attempts on my life, I counted these down and there was only one left. Later on, people would call this my Passion.

I was a target my whole life; inside mum's womb, through my first breaths, and right through adulthood. I experienced the full force of evil, but it was friends turning their back on me that hurt the most. From the political elite to the religious establishment, they all wanted me dead. This was written about me and sums up my life:

"Who, being in very nature God, did not consider equality with God something to be used to his own advantage; rather, he made himself nothing by taking the very nature of a servant, being made in human likeness. And being found in appearance as a man, he humbled himself by becoming obedient to death — even death on a cross!"[109]

Jesus was not married, but metaphorically, and spiritually we see the intimacy between God and Israel as a marriage. Hosea paints a tragic picture of the divorce between Israel and God. We wonder why God is so passionate about marriage, I think it's because he's lived through the rejection, hurt and humiliation of a divorce. He understands the pain of separation and has been left heartbroken.

Jesus was a family man. We're given little insight of Jesus' earthly family, but Matthew provides his brothers names; James, Joseph, Simon, and Judas. We're not given names for his sisters, but as the plural is used, there's at least two. Jesus had a minimum of six siblings. As the older brother, and with the mystery surrounding the fate of Joseph, it's likely Jesus took on some parental duties in the home as an aide to Mary in raising a large family. Some time later we read Jesus experiencing tension within his family:

"When his family heard about this, they went to take charge of him, for they said, 'He is out of his mind.'"[110]

There's debate as to whether *his family* relates to blood family or those in a close relationship. Still, there's nothing as dispiriting as those closest to you pulling you down and calling you *"out of your mind."* People in awkward family situations can take comfort in knowing Jesus also experienced family tension. John continues this theme

"For even his own brothers did not believe in him."[111]

God is not immune to the trials of family life.

Turning again to how Jesus' auto-biography could read:

Through my arrest and trial, I was considered worthless, and of no value. A Passover custom allowed the release of a prisoner; there were only two to choose from; Barabbas was the other choice, and they chose him. I faced Pontius Pilate and he was a hard man to work out. His wife begged him to have nothing to do with me but all Pilate responded was *"I wash my hands of this man."* Pilate was no friend of my people, feared and was ruthless; Luke spoke of this

"Now there were some present at that time who told Jesus about the Galileans whose blood Pilate had mixed with their sacrifices"[112]

At least Pilate was alarmed at Barabbas being the peoples' choice. The mob was calling for my blood, and I knew my blood is what they'd get. I'd become lower than a prisoner of ill-repute. I'd become less than nothing, and an object people wanted to discard.

I do laugh sometimes at the irony in the proceedings of the day; I was a king accused of treason, held by soldiers with spears blinded to the full strength of my angelic nation mustered at the smallest of my requests. That would have been heaven invading earth. I knew, of course, I couldn't initiate this invasion. It must have been hard for the angels, though. Throughout eternity their lives had worshipped me, and now they silently listened to the abuse and insults being hurled at me by the creatures I'd created. This was confusing for them to understand; why didn't I use my authority?

My heavenly beauty was beyond compare, and now they saw me as a broken man. Bruised black and blue, and torn to pieces. They saw me humiliated. I often wonder if they'd drawn comparisons between the fall of Lucifer and the fall of Judas. Judas had less power but was allowed to hand me over to be killed.

To write that judicial, societal, and customary norms were ignored is an understatement. I was a guilty man, this is all the people wanted to hear.

Jesus understands us. He gets us because he's lived with us and experienced everything we could ever experience. Jesus has authentic empathy towards us; for those abused and alone, for those plagued by temptation, for those struggling as single parents, for victims of cruel systems, for those who see friends walk away, turn their backs and gossip, for those misrepresented or misunderstood, for the thousands falsely imprisoned through slavery or conviction. The internally displaced, and the refugee. Those going through the heartbreak of divorce, or seeing a close friend turn their back. Jesus gets us, and his empathy is genuine.

Jesus suffered more than we will ever know, or understand, yet we can be sure Jesus was no masochist. He pleaded for his life but willingly walked through suffering and turned his back on his natural urge of self-preservation. He was fully human and this ability to deny himself is perhaps one of Jesus' greatest accomplishments in the passion story.

Jesus' suffering was not limited to his few decades in human form. Revelation provides a glimpse of the Heavenly Realm, and in Chapter 4 we're carried to the unimaginable brilliance of Heaven's Throne, and meet John struggling for words to describe the sheer magnificence and awesome splendour of all he's experiencing. So magnificent was the appearance of God, and the atmosphere of the Throne, John could only find words describing the perimeters of his comprehension – jasper, carnelian, an emerald rainbow, 24 Elders, golden crowns, thunder and lightning, blazing spirits of God, a crystal sea, and creatures from another dimension; of Elders falling prostrate before the indescribable God. Moving through the Throne Room we see John overcome with emotion, John simply *"wept and wept."*[113] Stepping to the centre of this brilliance, we meet a lamb. But this is no ordinary lamb, describing this encounter John writes *"Then I saw a lamb, looking as if it had been slain, standing in the centre of the throne."*[114] Whereas John was overcome and unable to describe the features of God, managing only to describe God's exuberance; John does not struggle for words to describe Jesus, *"Then I saw a lamb, looking as if it had been slain."*[115]

Jesus carries his physical wounds in Heaven.

We dismissed any notion of Jesus being masochistic at his crucifixion and Philippians[116] tells us that he emptied himself of all pride, yet here we meet Jesus wearing his stripes for all of heaven to see; and quite a possibility for all eternity. Such was God's love for you and for me, he became scarred for life; when we look at Jesus, the slain lamb, his healing takes on fresh meaning. The angelic nation can look on Jesus and capture the transactional scars sealing the angelic rebellion once and for all, the devil can look on Jesus and be reminded daily that there's nothing he can offer Jesus that could ever come close to those scars, and Father can look at son – in his fullness – without the need for Jesus to appear without blemish or wrinkle.

There are no easy answers to why people suffer, and as we search for answers, we may end up with more questions. The one thing we can be sure of however is, whatever we suffer, God suffered more, and he did this as a volunteer.

I suggest that when it comes to pain and suffering God is a travel guide rather than a travel agent. He has walked the journey and has suffered greater than any human.

Chapter 17
The Modus Operandi of the Loving God

"God proved His love on the Cross. When Christ hung, and bled, and died, it was God saying to the world, 'I love you.'"

– Billy Graham [117]

When we look for God and search for who he is, there are three defining anchors that provide complete confidence for all we need to know about the person of God. These anchors can be seen as governing-metaphors, or root-metaphors representing the bottom-line in defining God. The first metaphor is Jesus. The second metaphor is God's declaration about himself in Exodus 34:6. The third metaphor is Holy Spirit.

Besides these root-metaphors, there's also evidence all around. Nature reflects the beauty of God, but nature is not God. The study of science and continuous scientific breakthroughs can reveal his universal laws at work, yet science is not God. The mysteries of the deep can allow us to fathom the wonders of God, yet mystery is not the fullness of God. We can see God at work in our lives, the fingerprint of God can be seen the globe over, yet his fingerprint is only the remnant of his character and nature. These factors speak of God, and these examples give testimony to where God has been, but they only represent the shadow or outpouring of God. If we focus only on the outpouring of God or the shadow of God, we'll only obtain a partial understanding of who God is, and miss the complete and true representation of God.

Focusing only on the outpouring of God leaves many gaps in the jigsaw puzzle of discovering God. Deep down and regardless of demographics and cultural inheritance, we all have the desire to seek and find the fullness of God. We have the desire to know God and to connect with the one who gave us life, and the one who calls us sons and daughters.

Beyond mere flesh and blood, the framework of our being includes spirit and soul and these two elements collectively cry out and yearn for a relationship with God. Relationship with God is where our story began. We have a natural and inbuilt desire to seek out this relationship, and when we fail to discover the completeness of God we fill the gaps with misguided views of God. We're left to fathom the mysteries of the creator of the universe through filters of prejudice, offence, unbelief and a myriad of perspectives developed through limited understanding. We replace God as the subject of our need to worship, with alternatives, leading to statements similar to 'why does God allow suffering?' We end up developing the warped versions of God discussed earlier; the War-God, the Karma-God, the Genie-God, etc.; versions of God derived from personal **doubt**, **fear**, and **entitlement**; any version of God besides the God of Love.

Perhaps this is what Judas did at the betrayal? He saw the wrong version of God and tried filling the gaps with a warped view. Writers have speculated on the motives of Judas ranging from Judas simply a self-absorbed thief, right through to Judas as a zealous nationalist compelled to force Jesus out of the shadows and into a corner, leaving Jesus no alternative other than to reveal his cards and come out fighting; to lead the uprising and revolt, and bring freedom from the Empire. Jesus: the ultimate War-God, sword in hand, rising from the shadows of deep-cover to conquer the forces of brutal occupation.

Whether a thief or a nationalist, one fact remains; Judas only saw the shadow of Jesus, leading to remorse without repentance, and despair leading to suicide. We do well when we seek the fullness of Christ.

The First Metaphor: Jesus "Immanuel" God With US

Jesus sheds undeniable light on God's character. Look at his life. Look at God on earth. We read how Jesus did get angry, but these were rare events. What made Jesus angry? What was the object of his anger? In a simple system of classification we see Jesus' anger directed towards:

1) Barriers to worship
2) Barriers to healthcare
3) Barriers to equality
4) Barriers to freedom

And generally speaking Jesus' anger was aimed at three types of people

1) Leaders of organised religion and holders of public office who placed legislation in front of love
2) Hypocrites, and
3) Satan

God is displayed for all the world to see through Jesus; the true representation of God.

I doubt the disciples could have survived three years with Jesus if his *modus operandi* was anger. If Jesus was tyrannical, if Jesus' character was not trust-worthy the gospels would read so very differently. The gospels speak of the early disciples' enthusiasm to drop everything and follow Jesus, I consider this would have been a spirit-to-spirit conviction and not a heavy-handed, or coerced demand to follow. This resolute desire to drop everything and follow would be love-based and not fear-based.

An angry Jesus would most likely have been an angry child and known throughout the community, perhaps as the school bully and a child to avoid in the school yard.

We know precious little about the early life of Jesus and afforded only the rarest glimpses into his adolescence and upbringing. God does not cover up questionable characters in Jesus family line; murderers, and prostitutes to name a few. God reveals the good, the bad and the ugly. I don't think God would have hidden the school reports of Jesus, where in close-knit Jewish communities his reputation would have been known. We do read later how Jesus was not accepted in his hometown, but this is because of what he had grown to become; a prophet, and not because of historical misdemeanours and a bad reputation.

Angry people generally want revenge, are often self-justified and run countless scenarios in their minds of how they wished they could go back in time and say something different; or focus their minds, prepare and rehearse for future conflicts. Anger often turns to rebellion and aggression; or rejection, rendering them inadequate whilst building a profile of self-pity. If Jesus was angry with a tendency towards rebellion, or a tendency towards rejection I do not think he would have survived his three years of public ministry. Jesus would have struggled to engage with the growing crowds of people demanding his time, energy and attention. Jesus was not characteristically angry.

In one episode Jesus asked his disciples [118] who people say he is:

"Some say John the Baptist; others say Elijah; and still others, Jeremiah or one of the prophets." [119]

These names are highly revered; John the Baptist, Elijah, Jeremiah, or one of the other prophets. These are not names people would have chosen if they had not developed a high regard for Jesus.

Jesus continued:

"(but) who do you say I am", Simon Peter answered, *"You are the Messiah, the Son of the living God."* [120]

On one occasion disciples of John the Baptist were sent to enquire after Jesus, to learn his motives and report back on what they gathered. Jesus told them to return with the good news of healings and lives transformed. This is the introduction of Jesus; good news. There were many provocateurs in the life of Jesus who would have provoked an angry Jesus', yet:

- we do not see Jesus enraged by Peter's denial
- we do not see Jesus angered by Judas' betrayal
- Jesus keeps his silence during King Herod's mockery
- Jesus did not burn with rage during his torture at the hands of Roman soldiers

The anger of Jesus remained measured, withheld, controlled and rational; in contrast to his love which is beyond measure, is unconditional and transcends logic. The recipients of Jesus' unconditional love and acceptance included the poor, the downcast, the untouchables, prostitutes, tax collectors and sinners.

There's a long list of Biblical characters impacted by God's forgiveness

- Adam and Eve (original sinners) forgiven
- Cain (the first recorded murderer) offered forgiveness
- King David (adulterer and murderer) forgiven
- Peter (turned his back on Jesus and denied their friendship) forgiven

Compelling evidence, without any shadow of a doubt, God is love. He's not controlling or driven by rage, nor does He seek revenge. By contrast, God forgives rebellion, sin and wickedness.

Philippians[121] records how Jesus didn't consider himself (in earthly form) equal to God. Yet, we needed one of our own kind to redeem us; the second Adam. Jesus humbled himself, leaving all his power in Heaven's locker-room, and entered our human existence as a naked human baby; totally dependent, totally vulnerable, and needing protection by his human parents.

In summarising the fullness of God, we need only one word; love. Love is the foundation of God's Kingdom and provides the answer to every conceivable question. There's debate surrounding the question of why did God make humanity; my faith and conviction answers this in the simplest form; God is love and for love to be fulfilled it requires someone to love. Love needed a destination, and this is why God created Adam and Eve as intelligent creatures with the ability to respond to love out of choice. Love is the foundation of existence. It really is this simple. John captures this in his gospel and his first letter:

"For God so loved the world" [122]

"This is how we know what love is: Jesus Christ laid down his life for us" [123]

"Whoever does not love does not know God, because God is love" [124]

In the Garden of Eden, God did not give the 10-Commandments, he did not need to give a Bible with all its parables of wisdom, He simply gave his fullness; he gave Love.

When we read the Bible and review life, with all of its ups and downs, its trials and trepidations, times of peace and times of war, with the knowledge and confidence that God is love, life does make sense. By replacing *love* with *God* in Corinthians [125], we read:

"God is patient, God is kind. God does not envy, God does not boast, God is not proud. God does not dishonor others, God is not self-seeking, God is not easily angered, God keeps no record of wrongs. God does not delight in evil but rejoices with the truth. God always protects, God always trusts, God always hopes, God always perseveres. God never fails."

Isaiah prophesied the coming of Jesus and revealed the depth of God's love. He would take on the role of a sheep to be slaughtered by the hands of those he chooses to love. Meat Loaf famously sang '*I'd do anything for Love (but I won't do that)*' [126]; the heart song of Jesus would have been '*I'll give everything for love.*'

"He grew up before him like a tender shoot, and like a root out of dry ground.

He had no beauty or majesty to attract us to him, nothing in his appearance that we should desire him. He was despised and rejected by mankind, a man of suffering, and familiar with pain. Like one from whom people hide their faces he was despised, and we held him in low esteem.

Surely he took up our pain and bore our suffering, yet we considered him punished by God, stricken by him, and afflicted. But he was pierced for our transgressions, he was crushed for our iniquities; [127]

He was oppressed and afflicted, yet he did not open his mouth; he was led like a lamb to the slaughter, and as a sheep before its shearers is silent, so he did not open his mouth. By oppression and judgment he was taken away. Yet who of his generation protested?" [128]

Humanity's challenge in light of God's perfect love, is the devil's hate and the reality of evil. The devil turns purity of love into the demands of lust; replacing love with lust and freedom with anarchy.

It's dangerous to have freedom without limits. It's also a Catch 22 situation. My freedom to do what I want, when I want will clash with the freedom of someone else. It would see the rise of the tyrant, and the subjection of the weak.

Unfettered freedom would result in anarchy. Yet, the concept of freedom needing a framework, at first glance, appears contradictory; an oxymoron. Yet, it's necessary. The freedom of a spouse to drink all night and then abuse their partner is wrong and societies have laws to combat this behaviour. In this instance, the spouse's freedom would require freedom to be taken away from their partner.

A challenge of the 21st Century is how we perceive private rights and how we pursue private lives and private ownership. There is a difference between rights and freedom.

I've spent many hours and days driving European road networks; north and south, east and west. It's a fantastic system where the roads really do make Europe accessible; they are safe, well maintained and they allow for the European principle of freedom of movement and smooth access across borders. With relative ease we can visit ancient cities, we can be embraced with the magnificence of former empires, drive through glorious mountains piercing the sky, and visit some of the best beaches, lakes and coastal towns the world has to offer. We can travel during the day and we can travel at night, throughout every season in relative safety allowing travellers to come and go as they please. Yet what makes this freedom and safety possible is a set of rules and guidelines that govern our freedom.

This last statement presents an oxymoron *'rules and guidelines to govern our freedom.'* Rules and guidelines are needed to enhance the experience and maximise enjoyment. Road rules dictate what side of the road to drive on, how fast to drive, when to stop and when to start. They require appropriate driving based on the environment; implementing necessary changes for urban areas, school zones, construction areas and accident-prone areas. Yet it's the provision of rules and guidelines ensuring this freedom and opens up a whole world of adventure and exploration.

I no longer live in Europe and I may be painting a romanticised memory of driving through Europe, of adventures with parents on summer vacations or with groups crossing through to Eastern Europe in my later teens, yet within this framework is an analogy that proves helpful in giving some insight into God's plans for us; the need for a defining framework.

We need to pursue freedom in the framework of love. We need to respond to the freedom cries of those living under violent regimes. We need to respond to freedom-cries from those in slavery. We need to fight for those whose freedom has been taken away. Yet, if we consider that possibly they have been enslaved and their freedoms taken away because God has done this, then are we fighting against God in crying for their freedom. Can you get the sense of irony in this situation?

As Jesus-followers we have the mandate to engage this within the framework of love. It would be offensive if God were not angered; if Jesus was not angered by slavery, discrimination and inequality. As Jesus followers, we misrepresent God's character when we fail to respond with passionate anger and speak out against the wrongs of humanity.

The Second Metaphor: God's Auto-Biography (Exodus 34:6)

There are surprisingly few accounts in the Bible where we encounter

God speaking about himself in the first person; he speaks to others, he speaks about others, and he speaks about events and situations, but rarely does he make declarations concerning his character. We see this repeated in the life of Jesus who, as fully God, seldom declared his character speaking in the first person.

Exodus 34:6 is an exception, a foundational passage in our understanding of the character of God; a verse introducing his *modus operandi*. A verse we need to turn to when faced with the uncertainty of life and the mystery of faith, and whilst navigating challenging scripture. Those times when we need to know God.

We meet God introducing himself to Moses. It can be seen as God's autobiography. This is God talking.

"And he passed in front of Moses, proclaiming, "The Lord, the Lord, the compassionate and gracious God, slow to anger, abounding in love and faithfulness, maintaining love to thousands, and forgiving wickedness, rebellion and sin."" [129]

It's telling how this list is void of omni-statements. Over the years I've had many opportunities to be involved with groups where students have been asked to describe God in one or two words; 'creator', 'powerful', 'everywhere' always feature high on the list. And these attributes are correct. Yet, these are not the attributes God uses in describing himself. God chooses to focus on his character, those voluntary attributes, rather than the involuntary nature attributes – attributes that are unchangeable God, and the substance of who he is.

If all we knew, and all we're exposed to is the nature of God we may fail to meet the loving God. We need his character to reveal his love. In his involuntary nature, God is all powerful; he could kill us. God is everywhere; we have no escape. God is all knowing; he spies on us. God is eternal; we simply have no chance of escape. Yet by understanding his character we see God choosing to love, choosing to be kind, choosing compassion, and forgiveness. God chooses these attributes because he is deeply in love with us, and this is crucial in developing our relationship with God. God is not angry with us. God loves us.

The context of Exodus 34:6 reveals an authentic and compelling insight; a very intimate glimpse into God's love towards Moses. Throughout the wanderings of Israel, The Tent of Meeting became a focal point of God's intimate relationship with Moses and the nation of Israel. During the Exodus, Moses would pitch the Tent of Meeting some distance from the camp to meet with God:

"Anyone enquiring of the Lord would go to the tent of meeting outside the camp". [130]

Moses entering the Tent of Meeting was a very intimate affair,

"The Lord would speak to Moses face to face, as one speaks to a friend". [131]

Face-to-face intimacy is God's original desire for the relationship between God and humanity. We catch glimpses of this closeness in the Garden of Eden,

"Then the man and his wife heard the sound of the Lord God as he was walking in the garden in the cool of the day." [132]

There's no shadow of a doubt, God desires face-to-face intimacy. This intimacy was enjoyed with Adam and Eve, enjoyed with Moses, and promised in the Aaronic Blessing:

"the Lord make his face shine on you" [133]

God desires intimacy. Paul continues this theme in First Corinthians:

"For now we see only a reflection as in a mirror; then we shall see face to face." [134]

God's desire has been, remains, and will for all eternity be face-to-face intimacy.

Many falsely accuse God of being a harsh judge, they see a perspective of God and wrongly interpret it, or read about an action and draw a conclusion, or develop theology labelling God as vindictive and harsh. Exodus 34:6 provides a glimpse of the intimacy between Moses and God. Perhaps Moses was worthy of such intimacy, perhaps Moses deserved this special relationship.

Prior to God's Exodus 34 auto-biography, we meet Moses perched on a rock awaiting the arrival of God. God arrived; they spoke, culminating in two stone tablets inscribed by God with the words of the covenant; the Ten Commandments. Yet these were not the original stones. You see, in a moment of utter rage, Moses smashed the original stones to pieces. Travelling back to Exodus 32 introduces us to the rise and demise of the originals. Picture the scene.

Moses, the man selected as the people's advocate, prepares to climb Mt Sinai for a meeting to top all meetings; an audience with the creator of the Universe. This would be an event worth tweeting. Imagine the entirety of the angelic nation, both the good and the bad, waiting with bated breath, peering over each other's shoulders to maximise their view, to catch a glimpse of what is about to happen. Would this be a game changer? Hordes of the fallen kingdom with alert minds focused and poised with increased anxiety waiting to see what is to be revealed; preparing their legal mindsets, with zero grace and zero tolerance, conjuring all kinds of traps for humanity. As time progressed, movement happened. The meeting shifted towards closure, the finger of God began to inscribe the way forward for his beloved as captured on two stone tablets. Ten points were scribed. This is all that was needed; ten points to foster love and progress fallen humanity. Angels may have muttered, is this it?

At once, fallen angels began plotting how best to use these commands against Israel, whilst detail minded angels were busy looking for loopholes and traps, and considering addendums and fine-print that could be used by God's own children to one day stir passionate hatred towards God; to betray and accuse God, leading to false witness, false judgment, illegal conviction and incarceration, and ultimately the killing of God.

Can you imagine the scene? Can you imagine all that Moses must have been feeling? He'd met with God. He'd spoken with God. God spoke to him. He witnessed these same fingers that had flung the stars into space now begin to write with intimacy. Could he ever be the same again?

Some time later we meet Moses in a fit of rage smashing these stone tablets. In his anger, Moses had destroyed it all. The stones were beyond repair. Moses had destroyed the work of God. Exodus makes it clear that,

"The tablets were the work of God; the writing was the writing of God."[135]

How would Moses recover from this? The Karma-God would evoke a series of unfortunate events, bad karma, to inflict on Moses. The War-God may simply have snuffed Moses out of existence right there on the spot; whereas the Schizophrenic-God, well anything could happen.

I serve as a Board Member for a charity and an Incorporated Body, and as a Board Member, I know the importance of our founding documents; our Constitution, the by-laws governing our activities. These constitutions and other founding documents are precious and referred to when important organisational decisions are made. Board members change, but the founding documents are constant. The originals are kept safe, and working copies are made as a tool in meetings. As a Board, we do not have the authority to change our Constitution without approval.

These Constitutions are important but only to a limited scope. However, if I break the conditions of these constitutions, sanctions can be taken against me. I have a legal obligation to operate within their framework, and if I conduct myself in irresponsible ways, to no longer be 'Fit and Proper' I exclude myself from office.

There are many documents that hold importance in our lives; birth certificates, marriage certificates, and education certificates. Having spent over 12 years in immigration systems throughout the world, I do know the importance of keeping original copies. In a sense, they are the keys that have helped my family and me live and work in Africa, Asia, Europe, Australia and the Pacific, and by-and-large, it's the safe-keeping of these foundational documents that has opened the doors to many nations.

Our home nations have founding documents that guide and shape society, and at the global level, we have bodies to represent us and regulate our affairs. Again, these international bodies are instituted by founding documents. Generally speaking, the higher the body, the greater the significance of its founding documents over the conduct of our lives. When the Lord, when the creator of the Universe personally inscribes the Covenant for the Nation of Israel, one would assume this to be important, almost sacred; then we read of Moses tearing up this covenant. If our view of God is one of revenge, judgment and tyrannical behaviour we have to remain confronted with God's shocking response. What did the God of love say, perhaps something similar to this: *'let's start over Moses, take a few deep breaths steady yourself, come back up the mountain and we'll start again. But please, please take more care this time!'* This is stunning.

Whilst reading Exodus 34:6, we do well to remember this story of the original stone tablets, the anger of Moses and God's incredible response:

"And he passed in front of Moses, proclaiming, "The Lord, the Lord, the compassionate and gracious God, slow to anger, abounding in love and faithfulness, maintaining love to thousands, and forgiving wickedness, rebellion and sin." [136]

God's ordering of his attributes is revealing and becomes relevant in understanding challenging scripture and the chain-of-events leading to a questionable event. God is slow to anger, but to get to anger we go through compassion and grace. Beyond anger, we have boundless love, faithfulness and love again. We then read God forgives wickedness, rebellion and sin. It's only after forgiveness we learn how God does not leave the guilty unpunished:

"Yet he does not leave the guilty unpunished; he punishes the children and their children for the sin of the parents to the third and fourth generation." [137]

These are harsh words, and if God is simply our buddy we'll either ignore this warning or lose faith and find another buddy who just wants the good times.

The Third Metaphor: Holy Spirit

The fruit of the spirit; fruit that comes from God and fruit that reveals his character.

We need to speak and live the message of love, grace, reconciliation, and acceptance. Holy Spirit has been given to aid in this process. After Jesus' death and resurrection humanity was provided with the comforter and advocate; bearing fruit and gifts to build us up, and for the common good. Collectively they reveal the heart of God, providing confidence in his character: *love, joy, peace, forbearance, kindness, goodness, faithfulness, gentleness and self-control;* [138] wisdom, knowledge, faith, healing, miracles, prophecy, discernment, tongues, and interpretation of tongues.[139] Eighteen attributes; eighteen keys to personal identity, family harmony, regional development, national unity, and international diplomacy. These listings are void of words describing judgment, anger, or punishment.

Paul teaches that,

"against such things there is no law."[140]

The challenge of building an inaccurate or incomplete concept of God's love is that we can disregard the principle of the fear-of-the-Lord; a positive reality in our Christian faith. God does get angry, but we need to look at what makes him angry. Importantly, Exodus 34 reveals that God's anger is slow in coming.

Viewing Exodus 34 as a foundation of knowing God, and using the fruit detailed in Galatians 5 as a building block; we start to piece together the *modus operandi* of God. Exodus 34 reveals God's anger, albeit slow in coming, and Galatians 5 reveals how God's anger is salted with restraint and tolerance (forbearance), and is gentle and self-controlled.

The spirit is God, and the fruit of the spirit reveals God. It's noteworthy how the fruit introduces us to God's character, the voluntary choices of God, rather than his nature; the involuntary attributes of God. In nature, God is all-powerful, in character he chooses self-control. In nature, God is all-knowing, in character he chooses patience (forbearance).

Chapter 18
A Mystery of God

"The Lord looks down from heaven on all mankind to see if there are any who understand, any who seek God."

- Psalm 14:2 NIVUK [141]

There is scripture appearing to put God at the centre of death and massacre. How can this be?

A few days ago I found myself flicking through radio stations and stopped to listen to Rhema FM where Joyce Meyer was teaching; one of her points made an immediate connection:

"God's reputation in the world needs to be better" [142]

Whilst listening, it dawned on me very loudly and very clearly that in many instances God does have a poor reputation, and in many cultural settings this reputation is getting worse. I consider this to be a paradoxical statement, where opinion contradicts reality. It's not possible for God to have a bad reputation. God is good, God is kind, and God is love. How can we argue against this? I know this to be true, but how did we get from the serenity of Genesis 1 to the 21st Century where God's name is rejected and trashed by so many?

As I continued to listen, I started to wrestle with the questions *'why are we so silent?'*, *'Why are we not better advocates for the true reputation of God'?* I wonder if it's because we tend to avoid the tricky questions of faith as we're not equipped to answer them, or perhaps we wear a veil that allows us to quietly agree with those who question our faith, allowing the reputation of God to be construed through popular culture and the humanistic argument. Perhaps our identities are not secure enough to engage with a hurting world?

C.S. Lewis is a champion of faith. His books have touched millions and have made a deep impact on several generations. I'm gleaning from his thought-provoking book: *The Problem of Pain*. I love the *Chronicles of Narnia*, a favourite for some years with my sons; whilst *The Screwtape Letters* have had a profound impact on my understanding of the spiritual. Lewis is truly a master of promoting and defending the Christian faith be it through fantasy, or reflection. Yet, this ability of Lewis to advocate the true character of God took time to develop. Lewis rejected God and for many years was angry at God. Listen to how Lewis describes this period,

"My argument against God was that the universe seemed so cruel and unjust" [143]

Lewis viewed God through a veil, and the God being reflected back was inaccurate. Lewis' God was cruel and unjust.

We need to present God in his fullness, void of any veil. We do not need to defend God, he speaks for himself, but we do need to present a true image of God allowing others to form their opinion of God based on an unveiled portrayal; to promote and to advocate for God's good reputation.

There are, however, inherent challenges in presenting God who remains a mystery. How can we begin to fathom the mind of the creator of the Universe whose kingdom resides in a location that we cannot travel to? Whose kingdom is described as expanding on this earth yet remains unseen? Ezekiel paints a vivid word picture of God's kingdom descending on earth sounding more like a UFO occupied with creatures so far removed from our earthly animal kingdom that if painted would resemble more mythology than reality. Yet this is the Kingdom of God, the mystery of God, the Kingdom of Love.

In many ways, God remains beyond our ability to understand. His ways are not our ways. Isaiah simply writes:

"For my thoughts are not your thoughts, neither are your ways my

ways," declares the Lord. "As the heavens are higher than the earth, so are my ways higher than your ways and my thoughts than your thoughts."[144]

How to move beyond this position?

It's a mystery in itself that God who remains beyond our current ability to fully understand has made himself known in the simplest of forms; a fully dependent baby. A defenceless baby with total reliance on a mother and father to meet his every need, to show him love and acceptance, and to teach him right from wrong. Similar to the virgin in Isaiah who would be with child, who learned to reject the wrong and choose the right;[145] Jesus was a child needing to be taught how to live. Jesus' parents provided this nurturing environment allowing Jesus to grow in wisdom, stature, character and strength.[146]

If you've ever struggled with the battle for obedience, Jesus understands you:

"During the days of Jesus' life on earth, he offered up prayers and petitions with fervent cries and tears to the one who could save him from death, and he was heard because of his reverent submission. Son though he was, he learned obedience from what he suffered and, once made perfect, he became the source of eternal salvation for all who obey him and was designated by God to be high priest in the order of Melchizedek." [147]

An Invite to Take a Break

As this book continues we begin to dive a little deeper into the conquest of Canaan as a way to investigate God's love through challenging circumstances.

Will you keep walking with me through these pages? You could always stop here, grab a coffee and re-join me on page 142 but by doing so you'll miss the story of a stranger in a strange car in a sun-soaked land, Maori proverbs, the most mysterious man in the Bible, and stirring speeches by Churchill; if these aren't enough to fancy-your-curiosity how about the problem of allergic reactions and the unsettling work of the Holy Spirit. All pieced together with nuggets of gold, the missing dollar quandary and some tools to help navigate our questions. I hope you stay with me; or, enjoy the coffee and re-join me later for the story of an out-of-control barbeque, the question of what to do with old people, the art of hiding behind sofa's and da Vinci's perfect masterpiece.

The premise of this book is to promote the reputation of God and to identify the veils that spoil our view. The link is made between God's reputation and our identity; if we consider God's reputation to be poor we will always struggle with personal identity; yet, when we attain confidence in God's reputation we inherit the restoration of our identities. We desperately need confidence in God's good and perfect reputation.

The conquest of Canaan really is one of the most contentious parts of scripture. It recounts invasion, the displacement of nations and widespread carnage, leaving many commentators and observers wreathing at the God of the Bible. But we'll unpack Canaan and scratch around in the sand looking for evidence of God's love. The conquest of Canaan is an ancient event causing tremors through the 21st Century where the analogy of Canaan can be used as symbolism for our own personal insecurities and questions, our own personal hurts and the hurts of friends and relatives. In developing an understanding of God's actions in Canaan we also alleviate concerns of God being the War-God, the Angry-God, or the Schizophrenic-God.

It's important, however, how we form our questions. God is comfortable with our questions, yet we do have the responsibility to form questions from the position of a student rather than an accuser.

Chapter 19
Getting the Question Right

"Every ant knows the formula of its ant hill, every bee knows the formula of its beehive. They know it in their own way, not in our way. Only humankind does not know its formula."

- Fyodor Dostoyevsky [148]

Whilst the conquest of Canaan remains a reference point for many who look to discredit God and accuse God of anything other than *'love'*, God invites us on a journey of discovery to take a close look at Canaan and provides all the information we need to form our own opinions. Canaan is a challenging situation, but God wants the events of Canaan recorded for all to see; even in the face of accusation. We do not remove God from the equation of Canaan, but we do need to understand the equation, and time needs to be taken to form the right question, and to keep on asking.

God encourages our questions and even invites our doubts; not just on the historical events of Canaan, but our own personal doubts and questions that hinder our lives in the 21st Century. Yet the way we ask questions is important.

When we question God from the position of an accuser rather than a son or a daughter we shroud our relationship through wearing a veil. Or similar to a toddler constantly asking the *'why'* question without really wanting to know the answer.

For several years, I have to admit, I was stumped with the *Missing Dollar Riddle*; a riddle dating back to the 1930s dealing with the concept of *informal fallacy*; a situation where the combined components of an argument do not support the proposed conclusion.

Although the wording and specifics can alter, the riddle generally runs along these lines:

"Three men go to stay at a motel, and the man at the desk charges them $30.00 for a room. They split the cost ten dollars each. Later the manager tells the desk man that he overcharged the men, that the actual cost should have been $25.00. The manager gives the bellboy $5.00 and tells him to give it to the men.

The bellboy, however, decides to cheat the men and pockets $2.00, giving each of the men only one dollar.

Now each man has paid $9.00 to stay in the room and 3 x $9.00 = $27.00. The bellboy has pocketed $2.00. $27.00 + $2.00 = $29.00 - so where is the missing $1.00?" [149]

Perhaps you're now as confused as I had become, or perhaps unlike me, you did excel at high-school maths and you're able to raise your hand with the correct answer. After all, this is a riddle, and riddles exist to confuse.

You can do the research to gain a complete understanding of this riddle, but what remains important is how the answer is confused by the question. In the case of the *Missing Dollar*, there's no reason why the sum of components should be $30. It's only $30 dollars when we assume it to be $30 dollars, and by unpacking the components of the question we realise we're trying to make an answer out of the wrong question. The question is worded in such a way that it conceals what is going on and the question is fundamentally flawed. It can never reach an answer of $30.

The main takeaway from this riddle is to not accept everything we're told and to analyse the source of information. '*God is mean*' is a common statement, yet this assumption is fundamentally flawed. The statement, '*God is mean*', pieces together out-of-context components of understanding, and merges them together so as to form a wrong assumption. There's no equation in the whole world that could ever result in the answer '*God is mean*'. We can only reach the flawed conclusion '*God is mean*' by using flawed arguments, flawed assumptions and flawed opinions on the input side of the equation.

By placing God at the centre of Canaan – at the centre of suffering – fulfilling the role of the hurting and broken-hearted God, of a God in tears, we can start to understand the role of God in the unfolding story of humanity. God does take a position on pain and suffering, and we do have a secure anchor to neutralise any doubt in God's position on pain and suffering:

"In the beginning was the Word, and the Word was with God, and the Word was God. He was with God in the beginning ... The Word became flesh and made his dwelling among us." [150]

This text presents the most remarkable transaction of all time; God became flesh. As flesh, God reconciled the world to himself becoming the ultimate peace treaty; the forgiveness of sin, the hope of glory, and the promise of adoption into God's family. During this transaction, the flesh was torn beyond recognition and the flesh was nailed to a cross to suffer the most agonising of torture, humiliation and death. The flesh was God.

God did this as a demonstration of his love, holding nothing back. God became the peace-treaty between God and humanity, but not a peace treaty between God and the devil. There is no treaty to be had with the devil, and this is why it becomes so very important we choose God and not evil. Systems of evil will always be dismantled and demolished; the remaining inhabitants of Canaan clung to this system and suffered the foretold consequences of their decision.

At the end of the age when time ticks its last breath, there will be a form of reckoning, where evil will be removed and is no longer able to penetrate, and the establishment of the new heaven and new earth will begin [151]. We're provided little insight as to the location, or atmosphere of the new heaven, but we're provided with the most comforting of promises, and the smallest of glimpses:

"He will wipe every tear from their eyes. There will be no more death' or mourning or crying or pain, for the old order of things has passed

away." [152]

By investigating God's character in Canaan, I hope to build confidence in your identity and to build a solid foundation of God's good reputation; reputation and an identity standing strong in response to personal suffering and the pain of others.

As a disclaimer, I do have a heart of mercy, and I struggle with the conquest of Canaan. In my own understanding, I wish Canaan had not happened, and I struggle at times to defend God's actions in Canaan. I consider the nations of Canaan could have been blessed, and they could have lived as great benefactors of God's unconditional love, whilst taking their place in history as nations of great significance if only they listened to their hearts. Yet, I have a secure foundation that what happened, happened because the nations had rejected love and gone beyond the point of no return.

I do suggest that people in Canaan with soft hearts, hearts that could define the sanctity of human life had the opportunity to escape pre-conquest. Many Canaanites did flee, Joshua uncovered deserted cities and we'll look at Rahab as the last known person to flee Jericho. In contrast, those with hard hearts who had become entrenched in their practice would suffer the consequences of their life choices. It's perhaps a point of irony that by accusing God (of death and destruction in Canaan) we defend the human rights of people who developed and maintained sophisticated regimes of child abuse, torture, and horror on a national level.

Chapter 20
All Roads Lead to Canaan

"I cannot comfort him either; he has made himself unable to hear my voice. If I spoke to him, he would hear only growlings and roarings. Oh, Adam's son, how cleverly you defend yourself against all that might do you good!"

- C.S. Lewis, *The Magician's Nephew* [153]

This section is the one topic I was dreading to write and desperately wanting to avoid. On numerous occasions I allowed myself to contemplate writing this book without any mention of Canaan. I concluded this was not possible, however. Whilst writing, I had numerous conversations with people who loved this books concept but would remind me of the exceptions, with Canaan being the biggest. These conversations would generally come to, *'but God did destroy and kill, so how can you say otherwise.'*

I spent significant time researching the views and opinions held by many people on the issue of Canaan, and many do carry a strong anti-God narrative. I've included several of these quotes in the conversation below, as these quotes form the narrative of anger and accusation towards God; destroying God's reputation. In our own lives, we'd also be exposed to similar narratives; narratives that ridicule our faith, narratives that question our faith, and narratives allowing us to quietly question the motivations of God. These narratives have a two-fold effect; they ruin God's reputation and they shake our identity.

As you read, don't just consider Canaan – I use Canaan as a benchmark of opposition to God – but consider the areas in your own life that resemble similar characteristics to the story of Canaan. Many of these questions no doubt start with *'why'*; *'why did God allow'*, *'why didn't God stop'*, *'why did God give'*, *'why doesn't God help.'*

Needless-to-say, I found myself in a tough place with every road leading to Canaan. I felt mounting shadows of mystery shrouding my thoughts. Every road really did seem to lead to Canaan, yet the roads (constructed through values, ideologies, and actions) leading to Canaan were built by man; in the face of God's grace, compassion, mercy, love and long-suffering patience.

Many times I challenged myself with this question: *'in reviewing Canaan, can I maintain my simple hypothesis that God is love?'*

To progress, Canaan had become unavoidable. Canaan was a historical event, yet there are countless tragedies in the world today that raise similar questions as to the events surrounding Canaan. At a personal level, many face daily struggles putting God's love in the spotlight, and often in the firing-line. The same questions valid for Canaan are valid today.

21st Century opinion of Canaan may manifest in the War-God veil, or the Angry-God veil, even the Karma or Schizophrenic veils, where a wrong understanding of Canaan spoils the narrative of God's love and creates fissures in our personal identity.

A foundational principle of Canaan and the Old Testament is to remember that in the Garden, the genesis of where it all began was relationship. There was no written word, or Law, given to Adam and Eve; life was based on intimacy. When humanity fell and humans became each other's enemy it was necessary to implement a framework for society, yet this framework – including the Law – is not God, it does not represent the heart of God, and it was for our benefit, and was a direct response to our fall.

Chapter 21
Canaan: A Failed State and Beyond Redemption

"It seems as though mankind has forgotten the laws of its divine Saviour, Who preached love and forgiveness of injuries – and that men attribute the greatest merit to skill in killing one another – war and peace."

- Leo Tolstoy, *War and Peace* [154]

The conquest of Canaan is hard to digest, and can appear contrary to the character of God, yet Canaan symbolises all that had gone wrong with humanity. Many consider the nations of Canaan had reached a level taking them beyond redemption [155] and it's not easy to contemplate a society where death and destruction had become so rampant. The Bible offers limited insight as to the depths of this societal breakdown in Canaan, but what is recorded is severe:

- extreme cruelty
- child abuse and child sacrifice, including the public burning of infants in the name of Molech
- the practice of incest
- the practice of bestiality (crossing many physical safeguards by mating the human species with the animal kingdom)
- the slicing open of pregnant women

We may never know the full extent and the full reach of evil pre-conquest, but we can see the havoc of modern societies that have given collective societal power to a deity bent on destruction.

When searching historical characters epitomising evil, there are countless candidates, but many single out Adolf Hitler as one who subjected entire nations and races to immense suffering. Churchill wrote much about Hitler and spared no punches about the evil unleashed in Hitler:

"Amid the excitement of the election the exultant columns of the National Socialist Party filed past their leader in the pagan homage of a torchlight procession through the streets of Berlin. It had been a long struggle, difficult for foreigners, especially those who had not known the pangs of defeat, to comprehend. Adolf Hitler had at last arrived. But he was not alone. He had called from the depths of defeat the dark and savage furies latent in the most numerous, most serviceable, ruthless, contradictory, and ill-starred race in Europe. He had conjured up the fearful idol of an all-devouring Moloch of which he was the priest and incarnation. It is not within my scope to describe the inconceivable brutality and villainy by which this apparatus of hatred and tyranny had been fashioned and was now to be perfected. It is necessary, for the purpose of this account, only to present to the reader the new and fearful fact which had broken upon the still unwitting world: GERMANY UNDER HITLER, AND GERMANY ARMING." [156]

Of all gods mentioned in the Bible, Moloch (referred also as Molech) stands as a powerful and sinister force demanding society step into the oblivion of evil. Whether Churchill's observations were correct in Hitler being a pawn of Moloch, or whether he was referencing Moloch as a general analogy to the depths of evil Hitler had fallen remains speculative; be it either way, the point is valid. Evil was driving Hitler. The Canaanites worshipped this god Moloch, and throughout the lands of Canaan Moloch required human sacrifice, and over hundreds of years, countless children and adults were sacrificed to appease the god Moloch. The culture and system of human sacrifice were well established in Canaan, and it's this practice that in many ways captured God's anger towards the people of Canaan.

Canaan can be confusing, yet it remains paramount that we do not build an image of God, and a theology of the ways of God, on the event of Canaan. Life could appear much easier if the conquest of Canaan had not happened, or at least if it had not been included in the Old Testament for the world to see.

Canaan was a tragedy, but it was an avoidable tragedy, and this is the key to understanding Canaan. Canaan was avoidable.

In pondering the question; *did God have a perfect plan (including a geographical location) for every people group, tribe and nation,* my conviction is *'yes'*.

Adam and Eve were without nationality and without human lineage, and God had a plan for them. Through Abram, all nations, current and future, were to be blessed; and Israel's calling was to be a light drawing all nations to God. The Old Testament focuses on the calling of Israel, yet other nations would have their own calling.

Revelation paints a beautiful picture of God's love for all nations:

"After this I looked, and there before me was a great multitude that no one could count, from every nation, tribe, people and language, standing before the throne and before the Lamb. They were wearing white robes and were holding palm branches in their hands." [157]

Genesis starts with **all** people, and Revelation ends with **all** people. Between Genesis and Revelation, Jesus came for **all** people, and Holy Spirit is sent to **all** people. John 3:16, one of the most globally known passages of scripture:

"For God so loved the world that he gave his one and only Son, that whoever believes in him shall not perish but have eternal life." [158]

'Whoever,' simply meaning *'whoever,'* with countless examples showing God reaching the whoever:

- Before the world was flooded God sent salvation through Noah
- Before the destruction of Sodom and Gomorrah God sent salvation through Angelic Beings

- Before the destruction of Egypt God provided salvation for non-Jews to escape with the Exodus
- Ruth, a non-Jew, found salvation through her love towards Naomi
- Before the destruction of Nineveh God sent salvation through Jonah

God reaches out to every nation, every tribe, and every people group. He's an inclusive God. The nations of Canaan were created to be recipients of God's love, but through their actions, they rejected this position and chose a different posture ending in disaster. They were in the wrong place at the wrong time, and they suffered.

When faced with mystery, sometimes all we can do is cling to our faith and find peace in the reality that our minds cannot comprehend the fullness of God, and that God's mind is inconceivable to our finite thinking. Yet, it does remain challenging if we allow our questions to develop into accusations, or simply to ignore these questions and allow them to develop into fracture-lines disrupting our understanding of God.

Chapter 22
A Terrible Reality

> *"You were the seal of perfection, full of wisdom and perfect in beauty. You were in Eden, the garden of God; every precious stone adorned you... You were blameless in your ways from the day you were created till wickedness was found in you. Through your widespread trade you were filled with violence, and you sinned...Your heart became proud on account of your beauty, and you corrupted your wisdom because of your splendor. So I threw you to the earth; I made a spectacle of you before kings. By your many sins and dishonest trade you have desecrated your sanctuaries. So I made a fire come out from you, and it consumed you."*
>
> - Ezekiel 28:12-18 NIVUK [159]

The choice of turning from God is eternal and agonising. We spoke earlier of two opposing Kingdoms with two value systems; two ways to communicate, two visions for our lives, and two versions of a preferred future; one a Kingdom of light and the other a Kingdom of darkness. When we look at the events surrounding the conquest of Canaan, it begs the question; whose footprints are fresh in the sand? Do we see the fullness of life, or do we see death, robbery and destruction? God is inherently good and abounds in grace and compassion, whereas the devil is described well by Pope Paul VI in 1972 as,

"a terrible reality, mysterious and frightening." [160]

The events of Canaan are a terrible reality, but a reality that could have easily been avoided. It is not a myth, or simply a fairy-tale to help amplify moral and ethical choices.

There will be a response from God to eliminate evil, and the story of Canaan is a story of eliminating evil.

Genesis 3:15 provides the first account of God's promise of a future void of evil; God's redemption plan, the protoevangelium - the first recorded messianic prophecy spoken to the serpent. A global declaration of forgiveness and reconciliation delivered shortly after the fall of humanity; and this plan has unfolded.

The protoevangelium; God's victory speech delivered in advance:

"And I will put enmity between you and the woman, and between your offspring and hers; he will crush your head, and you will strike his heel."
[161]

We do know the enemy has already been defeated - after losing The Battle for Heaven, he lost The Battle at the Cross, and his future being foretold, we know he loses the final battle at the end of the age. Despite these loses he does remain active and present, and even though he is tethered he's tethered to a long leash. The benefit of the devil being on a leash, however, is that we can avoid potential danger by giving a wide berth.

Parents become apt at the subtle art of wide-berths. As parents raising sons who loved parks, my wife and I became very aware of the environment of the park. Our sons spent their early years in neighbourhoods where local play areas would often be littered with broken glass, the odd needle and all kinds of rubbish. As parents, we'd scan the environment and remove any danger. There'd often be people walking dogs; most of these dogs would be on a leash, but not all. We helped our sons determine what action to take if the dogs were not on leashes, how they should react and where to place their hands. We helped them realise that even a placid looking dog can snap if approached. In the spiritual, this is called discipleship, where we help each other make the right decision and avoid pitfalls.

Despite being on a leash the devil retains the ability to shout, and to influence whilst seeking hosts in his quest to extend the reach of his failed kingdom. When combined with his mastery of the art of cunning and deception, and mankind's need to blame someone for the world's wrongs, it's little wonder many people target their blame towards God. God also has a habit of remaining silent in the wake of accusation. This ability drove King Herod to the point of despair and Pontius Pilate to the point of amazement. They both had an intimate audience with God[162] and recounted accusations against God; and in the case of Herod, hoped to see a miracle performed. On the whole, God remained silent, punctuating this silence with the occasional '*if that's who you say I am*' statement bringing simplicity to the proceedings.[163]

The man Canaan (the grandson of Noah, son of Ham, and brother to Egypt, Put and Cush) was born after one of the greatest redemption stories of all time; Noah's Ark. Eight people entered the Ark,[164] and eight people disembarked the Ark stepping into a brave new world. These eight people represented humanity in its entirety; they were redeemed, they were loved and they were full of promise, and several nations occupying the land of Canaan trace their lineage and heritage to the man who carries the name Canaan; the Grandson of Noah.

There's no indication Noah and his family were preserved in the Ark simply to be cursed or doomed to failure. The Bible does not recount this and it's not in the character of God to operate outside the framework of love. These eight people, their children and their children's children, were loved beyond our wildest dreams by the Father of Love. God loved Canaan, there is no alternative conclusion.

Within this re-established world there remained freedom of choice. As the case with Adam and Eve, Noah and the remnant were presented with alternative kingdoms and free-will. Evil was not banished, and evil was present. Shortly after disembarking the Ark evil did take root again and the sin of man increased to frightening levels, infiltrating the nations of Canaan.

Why evil became intrinsically attached to this lineage is complex and may never be fully understood. Yet, with the premise that God will always bring evil to an end, combined with the distressing realisation that the nations of Canaan had collectively become entangled with evil, we see how the unfolding narrative was fast moving to its conclusion. Evil is more than a void of God, it's an active power bent on destruction, and once intertwined with Canaan, a power base inflicting cruelty on a terrifying scale was developed.

Evil is a greedy element desiring the world and not simply a region.

Herein lies the challenge. The Pentateuch[165] introduces us to ten nations occupying the land of Canaan;[166] yet this land of Canaan had been promised – or given – by God to Abram and to Abram's descendants. This is an ancient promise dating back to the narrative following the Abrahamic Covenant of Genesis 12.

Abram received this promise in Genesis[167] and this promise is renewed to Abram's son Isaac[168] and renewed again to Isaac's son Jacob.[169] This same promise is renewed and passed down through Moses to the people of Israel.[170] Included in this covenant are proselytes, people of the land[171] who turn to God; referred to as strangers, as sojourners in the land, or simply as newcomers. The word 'proselyte' can find much ill-favour in the modern setting, but within its original parameters it offered provision for people to be included in relationship with God; a provision for nations to become benefactors of God's fullness and to enter into a love relationship with God. The promised land was to become a sanctuary for not only Israel but the widow, the orphan, the downtrodden and those fleeing injustice. The origins of this provision can be seen with many non-Jews leaving with Moses at the Exodus from Egypt.

Israel was to be a welcoming nation, with a holy calling to defend the cause of the poor and to seek peace in the land, whilst developing strong and healthy relations with surrounding nations. This reflects the heart of God; to enter relationship with all people.

Israel was not to be a closed society, and Israel would fail in her purpose if she became a closed society. Foreigners were to be welcomed and God instructed Israel on how to interact with non-Jews:

- God reminded Israel to reflect on their time as captives[172]
- Israel was forbidden to mistreat strangers[173]
- All were to be regarded as equal under the Law of Israel; native-born and strangers[174]
- Foreigners were to be recipients of love[175]
- Worship of God was available to both Jews and non-Jews
- Non-Jews were invited to partake in the Sabbath,[176] invited to observe the Feast of Unleavened Bread,[177] and find forgiveness through the sacrificial system.[178]
- Non-Jews were welcomed to observe the Day of Atonement,[179] were invited to eat the Passover and to obey God's Law.[180]
- The full blessing of God was available for non-Jews

The bottom line; foreigners were welcomed, they were provided for, and received God's blessing. Israel was instructed not to mistreat the foreigner because Israel's God was a missional God, and Israel's calling was to reflect the heart of God.

The challenge, however, is nine words included in Genesis:

"At that time the Canaanites were in the land" [181]

This statement, *'Canaanites were in the land'* is an observation and void of any attitude towards the Canaanites. As we read through Genesis we catch glimpses of the relationship between Abram and the people of the land (the Canaanites), and this relationship is one of honour, respect and mutual agreement.[182] Yet, as the story unfolds we see how this original position of honour and respect became one of military engagement and the conquest of Canaan.

Were the inhabitants of Canaan aware of the promise of God to Abram? To this question, I do conclude the answer to be 'yes'. Abram was called to Canaan and had walked and lived amongst the Canaanites.[183] Answering yes to this question helps understand Canaan through the eyes of a loving Father with a soft-heart. We know Abram as a righteous man[184] and his witness would have impacted on the people of the land.

Several years back I was part of a team spending time in a nation suffering significant challenges; crime was high, vigilante law was rife and the power of the state was limited.

I arrived several days after the team had settled in; the nation was tense with two leaders claiming one position as head of government. Army units were fighting police units and institutions were aligning with one of the two presumed leaders. We were hosted by a most beautiful and caring couple; a considerable commitment as we were a group of ten. Like many cultures, our crowd was drawing a wider crowd and we were soon sharing the house with extended family and friends. Space was tight yet we were thankful for a door with a lock, for running water and even though the house was small we found space each night to lay down a mat to sleep.

The days were exceptionally hot and humid, and it was one of these days that a car pulled into the compound. A local man with a hostile demeanour jumped from the car and without delay engaged our hosts in a heated conversation. At the end of this brief encounter the man sped off, leaving our hosts to report that the stranger worked for the landlord, and the landlord had not approved our temporary visit. More importantly that he would soon return to implement our eviction. With little time for questions or without fully understanding the situation, we could tell in the eyes of our hosts this was a serious situation and we should leave without delay, and within the hour.

We quickly explained this predicament to our group, and with no time for questions we gave a brief instruction; *'go back inside, pack your bags and be ready to leave within the hour'*. A commitment was made that we'd find shelter by nightfall, and we were gone.

In this culture, our hosts were aware that disputes are rarely settled through regular authorities; rather, disputes were often resolved through a show of force and occasionally a stash of weapons. We needed to leave as the threat against us was real and it was overpowering.

We were foreigners in a foreign land, ignorant of local customs and arrangements. We were unaware we'd caused offence. A few nights earlier we were thanking God for this provision of housing. Yet here we were, in the wrong place at the wrong time and in danger. We heeded the call and left. On a scale of imminent danger, we were close to the edge. In our defence, we were ignorant to the situation and if we'd suffered physical harm we'd consider this unfair, unprovoked and unjust. We'd received no prior warning nor had we any inclination of doing wrong. We were unaware of cultural norms and our hearts were to bless the nation and not to cause offence. If we'd received increasing warnings the story would have been so very different.

Perhaps this progression may have started with the landlord coming over for coffee and sharing stories, spending time getting to know each other, and through this relationship we would have soon learned we were breaking tenancy agreements and that it would be good for us to move within a week or two.

In this scenario, we may have shook hands and bid farewell but refused to move. Subsequent visits by the landlord's agents became more frequent, and higher levels of disgruntlement were fast replacing chit-chat and our resolve to stay was increasing. We were entering dangerous territory and digging in. Time was passing and all warnings were being ignored. We now arrive on that afternoon in the blazing heat where the stranger in the strange car pulled into the compound carrying a final warning of imminent danger. The landlord is coming, he'll have his band-of-men and only one option remains; force. As foreigners, this would have been a foolish outcome to not comply with local traditions and expectations. I'm sure there would have been a shock at what could have happened to us, but any investigation would keep returning to that one defining question; why on earth did we stay?

God had a good plan and a worthy purpose for the nations of Canaan with inheritance at their disposal, and where land (their own promised land) would have been allocated to them. Land allocation is important to God and we can read of God's desire for the post-flood world to be repopulated through 70 founders of nations described in the 'Table of

Nations.'[185] The Matthew Henry commentary provides useful insight as to the relationship between God, man and land-allocation:

"He has made the nations of men, not only all men in the nations, but as nations in their political capacity; he is their founder, and disposed them into communities for their mutual preservation and benefit. He made them all of one blood, of one and the same nature; he fashions their heart alike. Descended from one and the same common ancestor, in Adam they are all akin, so they are in Noah, that hereby they might be engaged in mutual affection and assistance, as fellow-creatures and brethren.

He hath made them to dwell on all the face of the earth, which, as a bountiful benefactor, he has given, with all its fulness, to the children of men. He made them not to live in one place, but to be dispersed over all the earth; one nation therefore ought not to look with contempt upon another, as the Greeks did upon all other nations; for those on all the face of the earth are of the same blood." [186]

God had been calling the inhabitants of Canaan to change for a very long time, and he didn't just send one voice at the very last minute, he'd been reaching out to Canaan for centuries:

- Was it God's plan for these nations to spend time in the Promised Land but to leave before Israel arrived?
- For these nations to pass through as nomads?
- Had they been allotted their own promised land elsewhere but flatly refused God's invite and provision?
- Should the land have been vacant with no need for war and destruction?

We may never fully know the answer to these questions, or the events leading to Canaan's settlement pre-conquest, but we can be sure that these nations had wandered very far from God's blessing, and we can be absolute that God exhausted every option to get their attention. God was patient and showing every form of restraint whilst desperately calling out to Canaan to change their ways and reject evil.

Effectively, the actions of the Canaanite nations challenged God's ownership of the land and the promise of redemption for humanity. They had planted their flag and failed to heed the warning of coming doom.

If the nations had heeded God's many warnings the story would be different. This really is about righteousness, fulfilment of promise and the protection of humanity, set in an ancient context so far removed from our experience in the 21st Century that it's sometimes hard to fathom. Yet this ancient account of ancient people continues to cause confusion and insecurity amongst many believers; and anger towards, and ignorance of God.

Before crossing over to Canaan we desperately need to see God in the fullness of his complete context. Having the complete context of God is important, and without this full picture, we're prone to forming opinions of God outside of relationship. We see God's shadow and construct misinformed conclusions about his character, and in forming these wrong conclusions we veil our relationship with God to our own detriment. Remember the three Governing-Metaphors discussed earlier; Exodus 34:6, the man Jesus, and the priorities of the Holy Spirit? Keep hold of these metaphors as we explore deeper.

To further develop our understanding of God, we'll look at the *Principle of First Mention* and the *Process of Increased Warnings* as valuable tools helping to navigate this wider context, and to grasp the bigger picture of the fullness of God.

The Principle of First Mention

This principle looks at the progressive development of a thought, concept, or idea; of actions and statements found in the Bible and to source them back to their first mention and original meaning. As a rule of thumb, teaching will have its roots in Genesis. Once the original meaning has been identified the reader can apply this meaning to the scripture in question to gain full understanding.

The first mention would characteristically be a simple understanding, and when a principle remains complex we may need to dig deeper until complexity is replaced with simplicity. Viewing situations without full understanding can be seen as a microscopic approach where we're searching through the smallest of cracks. The principle of the first mention provides a panoramic perspective, whilst retaining the ability to search the microscopic; akin to a cinematic approach with technicians using a range of equipment for panning, wide shots and close-ups.

God helps with this investigation by providing a chronological account of necessary history, complete with key dates, names and themes, all the way back to Genesis. This investigation can take time, and can become confusing as the journey backwards passes through Canaan, ancient cultural norms, and passes through centuries of detail and law raising a myriad of questions. We need to travel through these periods of time, however, to gain a full understanding of redemption and reconciliation.

This journey to the first mention reveals how far humanity had rejected God, the depths God took to draw us back, and how we needed a saviour. We're inquisitive creatures and tracing our history to the first of our kind meets our need to be complete. We want to know who we are, why we're here, and where we came from; this is natural for us, and God provides the means to attain security in our identity.

The origin of our story is simple; God loves us and God was pleased to create us. God went through the same life changing amazement and sense of awe experienced by any new parent at the birth of their child. We are co-created; our human parents giving our genetic make-up and physical attributes, whilst God gives spirit. Our physical bodies will reflect our parents, whilst our spirit will reflect God. God truly is our Father. He called my family tree *'very good'*, and this is quite the compliment from the creator of the universe

> *"Then God said, "Let us make mankind in our image, in our likeness… God blessed them and said to them, "Be fruitful and increase in number… God saw all that he had made, and it was very good."*[187]

Navigating backwards should fill our lives with love and hope, and if we quit half way through – or we fail to start – pure love can be veiled by **doubt, fear** and **entitlement**.

The first mention of God's relationship with humanity is seen with God looking upon Adam and Eve and with great joy, declaring us 'very-good'. This is the first mention of God's emotional response to humanity; we are very good and God is delighted with us.

Over the years something tragic happened in this relationship and we now meet the people of Canaan existing in an environment at polar extremes to a very good relationship with God. Something changed; either God changed or humanity changed. God's love never changes;[188] his love is the same yesterday, today and forever.[189] This principle of God's first response to humanity being 'very good' provides an unmovable anchor when we investigate all that went wrong with Canaan. The phrase 'very-good' provides the principle of the first mention when investigating God's relationship with us. God is good and God declared humanity 'very-good'; on the other hand, humanity rejected God, distanced ourselves, took on the nature of evil, and rebelled against God's love. Simply put, we fell.

The early earth was impacted by this fall of humanity, and the shockwaves of this fall have reverberated and devastated every culture and generation since. Each challenge and tension we face has its origin in this rebellion where Adam and Eve turned their backs on God. God's reply was to initiate redemption and we can follow the progression of redemptions story and learn of humanity's hit-and-miss response to God's love. We see this through the age of the patriarchs, we can discover the integral role of the sacrificial system, we are introduced to the Law and how the Law became a flash-light helping generations safely navigate the minefield of fallen humanity. We see how redemption progressed through the Judges, and through the highs and lows of the age of the Kings. We can learn how God provided prophet after prophet to bring clarity and instruction on living with God, right through to the killing of God (at the crucifixion of Jesus), and the sending of the Spirit.

God's character is to show mercy, grace and compassion. He will extend judgment, but this judgment is slow in coming and is avoidable for the individual. In Genesis, God spoke of Cain being cursed by the evil he allowed to form within his identity, yet this was Cain's choice. Prior to Cain killing Abel, God speaks:

"Then the Lord said to Cain, 'Why are you angry? Why is your face downcast? If you do what is right, will you not be accepted? But if you do not do what is right, sin is crouching at your door; it desires to have you, but you must rule over it'." [190]

Cain opened himself to the sin knocking on his hearts' door, and Cain allowed sin to infiltrate his identity. The God of love, however, continued his pursuit of Cain, and warning him one last time God spoke:

"sin is crouching at your door; it desires to have you."

In these words, we see the end of a process of increased warnings.

Process of Increased Warnings

In *"The Whole Story of the Bible in 16 Verses"* Bruno offers the following on developing a worldview shaped and moulded by the right understanding of God:

"Our view of the world begins with our view of God. The way we think about God shapes the way we think about everything else, along with the way we act and respond to every circumstance. Because of this, we need to get our thoughts about God straight at the beginning of our journey." [191]

We need confidence that eternity with God will be void of evil, and to get to this future position, evil needs to be eradicated, and the only way to eradicate evil is through the intervention of God. Yet true to God's character of being slow to anger and of providing endless mercy for all who will listen there will always be a process. A process looking similar to:

- God makes known the requirements of life and life to the full

- God makes known the danger of sin
- A formal set of instructions may be issued
- A first warning will be issued
- A succession of increasingly stronger warnings issued
- Minor discipline will be extended
- Moderate discipline will follow
- Increasingly progressive discipline follows
- Ultimately leading to death

This final result of death does seem harsh and appears to run contrary to the love of God. Yet the people would already be dead in their sins through their free-will; their freedom of choice to walk a path rejecting God's opportunities, warnings and sanctions to turn back to love. Turning to God became their only escape from inevitable death and separation. God starts this process with a little nudge, and with each escalation he provides redemption.

The land of Canaan, the land promised to Abram and his descendants, and the land chosen to bring forth Messiah had become, without a doubt, evil.

Acute evil had penetrated the land and the land itself had become cursed.

By placing God's patience under a microscope, and reviewing the events leading up to Canaan we witness God's character and his long-suffering, and we see God using many and varied methods to reach out to Canaan. God loved the people of Canaan with an unending love and his desire to see them redeemed from evil provides evidence, over hundreds of years, of God's character being slow to anger, God's pure tolerance, and his long suffering.

Chapter 23
A Brief History of the Future

"ka mura, ka muri"

ka mura, ka muri is a Maori proverb simply meaning *"walking backwards into the future."* It speaks of an important aspect of life; remembrance. Or, put another way, the perils of forgetfulness. Deuteronomy addresses this principle:

"Only be careful, and watch yourselves closely so that you do not forget the things your eyes have seen or let them fade from your heart as long as you live. Teach them to your children and to their children after them." [192]

Remembrance was an integral part of Jewish devotion to Yahweh, where God initiated festivals, advocated for shrines, and the setting up of standing stones for the advancement of memory. Jews were required to partake in ritual and daily meditation on God's goodness, and remembrance was central to Israel's identity.

When Israel became forgetful, they strayed. This simple equation *forgetfulness = straying* runs a current theme through the Bible, and God places a high value on remembrance; remembering the relationships, remembering the events and remembering circumstances.

Arriving on the banks of the Jordan and looking towards Jericho, we do well to cross the Jordan, as it were, backwards; being informed of the events that brought both sides of the conquest to their positions. To walk backwards into the future is to consider Jericho through the lens of God's character.

The *Principle of First Mention* and the *Process of Increasing Warnings* become significant when looking at Canaan and learning of the events leading to the conquest. We do not remove God from the equation; rather, we seek to discover the love behind the action. At first glance, this seems a tall order.

A whirlwind had been brewing, and blowing down on Canaan for years, hundreds of years. Prior to the conquest, the nations of Canaan had countless opportunities to acknowledge and turn to God's amazing grace, his unending compassion, and his mercy and forgiveness. Yet sadly many Canaanites clung to evil, and the following seven points highlight some of the obvious opportunities Canaan had to turn from evil. Identifying these opportunities remain important to understanding the process of increased warnings and the long-suffering of God:

1. Israel's 400 Years of slavery in Egypt: in Genesis[193] we witness God speaking in dramatic fashion to Abram, foretelling Israel's 400 years of captivity in Egypt. Israel's captivity provided four centuries for the nations inhabiting Canaan to be the recipients of God's grace and God's warning. Israel was holed up, not able to move and take possession of the Promised-Land, and Canaan had 400 years to respond to God.

2. Leaving Egypt: Israel departed Egypt in a blaze of glory. Few events in the history of humanity will come close to the events leading to Israel's departure; the awesome and frightening power of God on display for all to see. Upon leaving Egypt, God kept Israel away from the relatively short journey between Egypt and Canaan; a journey of but a few days[194] instead, leading them by the *'Way of the Wilderness.'*[195] This decision provided an additional 40 years of grace for Canaan to respond to God.

Exodus provides insight into this decision *"If they face war, they might change their minds and return to Egypt."*[196] The inclusion of '*if*' at the outset of this rationale gives great insight to God's character and affords the opportunity to investigate how the conquest could have been avoided.

Was the exodus desert wandering all about Israel's preparedness? Or could it have been as much about Canaan's deliverance, in providing ample time for grace and mercy to penetrate Canaan? With trade-routes, the presence of nomadic tribes and a highly oral society, it's not much stretch of the imagination to consider reports of the exodus filtering through to Canaan. This flow of information would be made all the more expedient due to the developed highway system between Egypt and Canaan. Again, Canaan had time and they had advance notice.

3. Destruction of the Egyptian Army: the role of alliances, the importance of trade and commerce, and geopolitical knowledge were important in 1446BC. Egypt was a dominant military and political force in the region, and when a dominant power loses its army in one dramatic event regional players would have taken note. They would have wanted to know where the army fell, where the army was headed, and to whom the army succumbed to defeat. Reports would have filtered through that Israel was a major player in Egypt's defeat; the defeat of the mighty Egyptian army whilst pursuing a nation of slaves would have sent shockwaves through the region.

Canaan would have been aware of military movements and dramatic shifts in the geopolitical landscape so as to form their own response.

4. Miracles: Terrifying plagues, marvellous miracles, the destruction of a powerful army, and one of the greatest movements of humanity took place within close proximity to Canaan. Israel was not moving covertly, they stood out and were obvious; a rag-tag nation of slaves held together by miracle upon miracle. Canaan would have been aware of the miracles of the Red Sea crossing, the provision of manna, the display of fire at night and a pillar of cloud by day guiding Israel.

5. Israel was on the move: although it took 40 years of wanderings, Israel was headed to Canaan and Israel's delay provided an additional 40 years for Canaan to change their ways.

The Book of Numbers provides a glimpse into the relationship between God and Moses, and by chapter 14 we meet Moses pleading with God not to let his power appear weak in the sight of the nations:

"Moses said to the Lord, "Then the Egyptians will hear about it! By your power you brought these people up from among them. And they will

tell the inhabitants of this land about it. They have already heard that you, Lord, are with these people and that you, Lord, have been seen face to face, that your cloud stays over them, and that you go before them in a pillar of cloud by day and a pillar of fire by night."[197]

Egypt is the only named nation in this verse, yet the verse speaks of the *"inhabitants of the land"* and observations made by Egypt would be similar to the observations made by Canaan.

Rather than a sleek military machine, this human movement was well-advertised and painfully slow. God, through highly visible miracles, led the way. I'm not sure how high the pillar of cloud that guided Israel would have been during the day, and I'm not sure if the fire guiding Israel by night would have been visible along the borders of Canaan; perhaps at times and on a clear night, the fire may have been visible from the northern Highway and distant lands. What we can be sure of, however, is that Canaan would have been aware of Israel's movements. Over 440 years of extended grace for Canaan to turn from evil.

6. The Jordan Crossing: God had been working for hundreds of years to attract the attention of Canaan, and His patience was enduring. Many Canaanites would have responded to God – because God's word never returns null and void[198] – yet the structures of Canaanite society remained intact. Canaan not only posed a real threat to Israel but posed an increasing threat to regional stability. The story of the miracle at the Red Sea would no doubt be known in Canaan and Jericho. There may have been speculation and doubt on the validity of the story; had the story grown in exaggeration over the years, a little like the legend of Robin Hood from my home city. Was it simply enemy tactics to bring fear to the camp? Jericho, however, was to be provided evidence beyond any shadow of a doubt. Just as Moses raised his arms and the Red Sea parted,[199] Joshua would now mimic this crossing with God displaying his great power on the doorstep of Jericho. The Bible recounts how the waters of the Jordan (which at the time were in flood season) *"stood and rose up in a heap"*[200] with commentators suggesting a 30-mile stretch of the river bed being left dry.

This re-enactment of the Red Sea crossing, although in its own right a new miracle for a new generation did provide real concrete evidence to Jericho that God is coming. Canaan still had time to change the course of their history.

7. Marching round Jericho: The classic view of Israel marching around Jericho is a display of strength on Israel's behalf; and an opportunity for Israel to rally under the banner and to beat the war drum. Yet, could it also have been to keep Israel occupied for six more days, whilst the final call of mercy and grace reverberated within the walls of Jericho? Akin to the classic movie scene where a midwife provides a seemingly important task to a fumbling husband by asking him to run around and find hot water and towels.

Would this marching military confirm the numerous times the prophets, the angelic, and the 'stranger' may have visited Jericho to warn against this event unfolding before the city? The prophecies, the stories, and the yearning of the inner soul over the years would point to one awesome truth; God is real and God is here. During this period in history, people generally believed gods were geographically bound and would not venture into the territory of another god. For God Almighty to turn up on Canaan's borders would have been without precedence – a God who crosses geographical boundaries. Yet here his is standing on the river bank knocking one final to time on the hearts to all who will listen.

Israel spent six days marching, then with a heart full of grief and sorrow, God released Israel from their circular marching and wept at the outcome.

Four centuries, four decades and six days for grace to be noticed. Many Canaanites ignored this grace, but some responded to the work of God.

Rahab is the only case-study of God's interaction with a citizen of Jericho moments before destruction. We know little of Rahab's history but we're given insight as to her occupation, leading many to believe she was involved in some form of prostitution. Was she a victim of a brutal regime and forced into her occupation, or was prostitution the only perceived way she could support her family? Her history may have been glanced over, but her future is celebrated.

There was a passing of time between Rahab assisting the spies and the Fall of Jericho, providing time for Rahab to confront any personal doubts, to become re-occupied with the culture of the day and to sell her knowledge for the provision of reward. This would have been a true test of Rahab's faith; the promise of redemption in the midst of despair. The hope Rahab found in God, in contrast to the brokenness of Canaanite society provides an intimate insight into the decision-making environment of the last known Canaanite to vacate Jericho. Rahab contrasted two kingdoms; the Kingdom of Darkness where she lived with her family, and the Kingdom of Heaven that existed only in her young faith.

This gap in time would provide an opportunity for all occupants of Jericho to contemplate life, assess personal values, whilst considering family protection. There are varying timelines covering Joshua's conquest of Canaan, yet it's commonly agreed that the conquest happened over seven years (around 1400BC); seven years is a long time for the people of Canaan to turn to God.

As Joshua and his army entered Jericho they entered with hearts turned towards Rahab and for the redemption of those who made it into the '*Ark*' of Rahab's dwelling. In the height of the battle, God was delivering redemption to the last moment. This is not the picture of a God hell-bent on destruction and revenge.

We may have many questions about God, and many have accusations towards God; however, he does not cover-up his family line. He reveals his family tree and puts it on public record for all to see:

"Salmon the father of Boaz, whose mother was Rahab,
Boaz the father of Obed, whose mother was Ruth,
Obed the father of Jesse,
and Jesse the father of King David.
David was the father of Solomon, whose mother had been Uriah's wife."[201]

The family line of Jesus is remarkable and reflects redemption and grace. God is happy to introduce us to his family and relatives, and reveals who he enjoys spending time with. God is comfortable to call Rahab family. God's not a remote-theology from a distant Kingdom, he's present and personable; we see this closeness in the life of the human man Jesus. In Jesus, the true image of God, we meet him socialising with the tax collector, the prostitute, the leper and those regarded in the first-century pecking order as being unclean.

The same hands that flung stars into space reached down to touch the leper.

Rahab, who still carried the title 'harlot' through the New Testament, is first introduced as a disreputable person from the Amorite nation. Yet, she became integral in the royal genealogy of Jesus. This not only speaks of God's unconditional love but also speaks of a way-out. Not all Jericho was destroyed. Through her actions, Rahab became knitted into the nation of Israel joining Tamar, Ruth and Bathsheba as foreign ancestors of Jesus.

On the one hand, we can empathise with those who are angry at God and claim God to be genocidal, or we can take the longer journey of discovering who God is. It really is remarkable that Rahab as a Canaanite was grafted into the genealogy of Jesus. The case for God's love grows convincingly stronger.

Lockyer suggests:

"Both Jewish and Christian writers have tried to prove that Rahab was a different woman from the one whom the Bible always speaks of as a 'harlot'. To them, it was abhorrent that such a disreputable person should be included in our Lord's genealogy, and by Paul, as a woman of faith, and so her story has been distorted in order to further a scheme of salvation based upon human goodness. Although man's sense of refinement may be shocked, the fact remains that Rahab, Tamar and Bathsheba were sinful women who were purged by God, and had their share in the royal line from which Jesus sprang" [202]

We may be uncomfortable with the conquest of Canaan, and how this challenges our own identity in God; what remains important, however, is the outcome of the nations of Canaan was yet to be written, and the Canaanites would scribe their immediate future.

As we progress, the case for God's love towards Canaan over the centuries takes a dramatic shift. Had God visited Canaan in person?

Chapter 24
God in Canaan

"No one has ever complained yet of being too much loved."

- Leo Tolstoy *War and Peace* [203]

Melchizedek is quite possibly the most mysterious of all Bible characters; he was the High Priest and remains a priest forever. He was King of Salem.[204] He personally knew Abram, and Abram saw fit to pay honour to him. His name means *"King of Righteousness"*[205] and *"King of Peace."*[206] He was without a family line, with no recorded mother and no recorded father. He is without beginning of days or end of life. He was great and resembled the Son of God. Melchizedek really was a man of mystery and many commentators suggest Melchizedek be an archetype Jesus, Jesus himself, or a physical manifestation of the Holy Spirit.

The conclusion of Melchizedek being Jesus is not without precedence. We're provided with the word *Christophany* to describe potential appearances of Messiah pre-dating the New Testament, and there are several besides Melchizedek:

- The angel who wrestled with Jacob is considered by many as Christ in physical form[207]
- The mysterious man who appears to Joshua and identifies himself as the *"the commander of the Lord's army,"*[208] is considered a manifestation of God
- The fourth man in the furnace in the book of Daniel is described in the following way *"and the form of the fourth is like the Son of God"* [209]

In the age old adage *'location, location, location'*; location really does become important. Melchizedek was the King of Salem, and Salem being an early name for Jerusalem was located in Canaan. God had planted either a physical manifestation of himself or a person resembling Jesus in the land of Canaan, many years before the Conquest. Melchizedek was blameless, pure and righteous, and he reached out to Canaan with a message of reconciliation and peace. Such was God's love for Canaan.

Whether Melchizedek and other examples are true Christophanies, whether they were archangels or other forms is not conclusive. Yet, what they provide is real and physical evidence beyond any shadow of a doubt that God put meat on the bones of Exodus 34:6. He not only claimed in words but demonstrated in form.

God will go to every length to woo our hearts. Isaiah provides insight as to the ways of God by opening up a debate on principles. King Hezekiah and his counsel have entered a binding agreement with death, and we meet God in the midst of this debate, where the dialogue climaxes with God promising to do away with death and offers redemption from Hezekiah's legal contract with death:

"You boast, "We have entered into a covenant with death, with the realm of the dead we have made an agreement. When an overwhelming scourge sweeps by, it cannot touch us, for we have made a lie our refuge and falsehood our hiding place." So this is what the Sovereign Lord says: "See, I lay a stone in Zion, a tested stone, a precious cornerstone for a sure foundation; the one who relies on it will never be stricken with panic. I will make justice the measuring line and righteousness the plumb line; hail will sweep away your refuge, the lie, and water will overflow your hiding place. Your covenant with death will be annulled; your agreement with the realm of the dead will not stand. When the overwhelming scourge sweeps by, you will be beaten down by it. As often as it comes it will carry you away; morning after morning, by day and by night, it will sweep through." [210]

Verse 15 provides the opening scene; with boasting we find King Hezekiah placing his confidence in death's ability to save them. Verse 16 reveals God's response to this perceived state of security. God counter-offers an alternative promise of well-being whilst affirming his role as a sure foundation. Through this dialogue God offers for King and counsel to move from reliance on death and move to blessing and reliance on God; a move towards justice and righteousness. God's offer of peace comes with a disclosure that their current refuge and hiding place (death) is going to be swept away.

Although this passage is perhaps more of a mockery and more of a rhetorical rebuff against Israel's foolish notion of future success through the forming of ill-conceived alliances with Egypt, it does provide a useful insight to the promises of God, particularly when they relate to God on the verge of Canaan. God is saying flee death and choose life. The nations of Canaan had entered a contract with death. Yet, God made every plea possible, over hundreds of years, to woo them back.

In our God made image, we do struggle with death and destruction, as this is what makes us human. We would, however, struggle beyond hope with the alternative. Canaan had a history of warnings, in line with God's character, yet they chose not to turn. For some reason, they were beyond the point of turning and were creating hell on earth.

Looking at the conquest of Canaan through a 21st Century framework of understanding remains a challenge, yet it's not a surprise to God, he chose to include the events of Canaan. God knew the questions and accusations that would come his way and would hinder his followers, yet the importance of preserving this written account of the history and to learn the lessons from these events is considered important by God. For this reason, we need to find a position of confidence with Canaan and we need to see Canaan within the broader plan of redemption.

The conquest of Canaan was not about the annihilation of nations; it was the destruction of systems of hatred established by the collective who'd allowed evil to become intertwined in the fabric of their society, making it increasingly hard to distinguish the separate elements. Canaan was a clash of spiritual kingdoms. The tragedy is that people clung to these systems of hatred and for reasons we can only speculate on, many chose not to let go. A little like a sailor clinging to the anchor of a sinking vessel even though the lifeboat is at hand and rescuers are pleading for him to leave the ship.

Yet, isn't God good? Doesn't God love? Isn't God kind and compassionate? Can we consider that the conquest of Canaan broke God's heart on so many levels? God doesn't want anyone to perish, not even one. But Colossians makes the link between death and personal sin; *"when you were dead in your sins."* [211] The Canaanites were dead before they had died, and the blame for this condition lies at the feet of the individual. Canaan knew of God, Canaan would have been aware of their sin, and yet Canaan refused to shift. Unfortunately, the fault of Canaan rests with the inhabitants of Canaan.

Chapter 25
The Unsettling Work of the Holy Spirit

"Now when all the Amorite kings west of the Jordan and all the Canaanite kings along the coast heard how the Lord had dried up the Jordan before the Israelites until they had crossed over, their hearts melted in fear and they no longer had the courage to face the Israelites."

- Joshua 5:1 NIVUK [212]

God knows our human frame well. He designed us and created us with three basic components; spirit, soul and body. As humans, we have access to the spirit of God, and the witness of the spirit over many years throughout Canaan would have been active in alerting the Canaanites to their current path leading to destruction.

As humans, we have a mind and we possess a conscience. Our conscience can be seen as an internal warning system, and God will utilise this spiritual sense to help guide us. When our bodies act against the moral code we inherit, our conscience will alert us. We intrinsically know when we do wrong and when we see others do wrong. Our conscience will cry out; it will alarm us, it will startle us, and it will bring discomfort. God will utilise our conscience as a way to get our attention; reacting with increasing levels of unease when confronted with evil. God speaks to our hearts, shakes our inner-core and disturbs our soul. Our bodies were never designed to host evil which is a force from a different dimension.

That's why we react at evil; as if it's an allergic reaction.

The nations of Canaan had gone beyond their conscience and were ignoring the inner cry of their soul and spirit. They reached the 11th hour and in pride kept marching with the bells of death ringing with increasing volume and ferocity. Their sensory conscience would have been on overdrive, with the feelings of fear and notions of being unsettled crying out. Their physical frames were operating contrary to the original design they were created for.

Evidence of the unsettling work of the Holy Spirit (in the internal battle of peoples' hearts) can be seen in none other than the King of Jericho, who began experiencing internal terror:

"The king of Jericho was told, "Look, Some of the Israelites have come here tonight to spy out the land"." [213]

In this narrative, a king is told of two men entering the house of a prostitute. What we know of Canaan is that sexual promiscuity was rife, and they were not a shy people when it came to pushing sexual boundaries.

For two men to enter the house of a female prostitute, in the climate of the day, was not uncommon. I wonder whether this news would be considered worthy enough to inform the King. Perhaps investigate with the Keeper-of-the-Watch, but not the king, unless the king was experiencing an acute internal struggle made all the more obvious through the confirmation of external happenings.

The King somehow knew danger was at hand, and perhaps knew he was being visited by another King. A little like the reaction of King Herod upon hearing news of a new King arriving in his territory at the birth of Jesus.[214]

Listen to Rahab's acknowledgement to Joshua on the state of Jericho:

"[Rahab] said to them, "I know that the LORD has given this land to you and that a great fear of you has fallen on us, so that all who live in this country are melting in fear because of you. We have heard how the Lord dried up the water of the Red Sea for you when you came out of Egypt, and what you did to Sihon and Og, the two kings of the Amorites east of the Jordan, whom you completely destroyed. When we heard of it, our heart's sank and everyone's courage failed because of you, for the LORD your God is God in heaven above and on the earth below". [215]

Rahab is confirming the spiritual condition of Jericho; *'we are shaken to the core, we are melting in fear, our hearts have sank, our courage has failed'*.

God was destroying a system of evil, yet liberation was available and for centuries God had been offering liberation. Even before Israel arrived on the banks of the Jordan, we read how *'all the people are melting in fear.'* [216] Many Canaanites, however, continued to ignore every opportunity and the consequences were fatal.

The book of Joshua introduces us to a well-known describer of Jericho:

"now Jericho was tightly shut-up" [217]

Although referring to the physical city, this would be an accurate diagnosis of the hearts of people living in Jericho, and throughout the land of Canaan. They were tightly shut-up; nothing came in and nothing came out beside their doomed lifestyles.

It's plausible to conclude the nations of Canaan had managed to remove themselves from salvation, where their entanglement with the devil had climaxed to such an extreme level their existence and their allegiance with the kingdom of darkness was now absolute and complete.

In the face of defeat, those remaining in Jericho and throughout the lands of Canaan were no doubt hijacked by the same pride that destroyed Lucifer.

The challenge of pride and greed working powerfully in unison is most likely the root of Jericho's fate. Greed jeopardised Adam and Eve's place in Eden. Whereas pride and greed were Lucifer's main weapons of choice at the failed tempting of God during Jesus' own desert experience. Pride is a powerful force.

God provided every opportunity for Canaan to change the course of their existence. How many heeded God's pleas we may never know, the

Bible hints that Canaanites may have departed, and that Canaanites were ready to leave as Israel entered deserted cities:

"In that day their strong cities, which they left because of the Israelites, will be like places abandoned to thickets and undergrowth."[218]

The narrative backdrop to Isaiah's prophecy resonated with the listeners of the day; where stories and written accounts of Israel uncovering abandoned cities were known. Years after the Conquest, Israel now faced a similar predicament of being invaded by the Assyrians. Isaiah speaks of this situation and draws a parallel between the Canaanites fleeing their cities at the onset of Israel's conquest and Israel now fleeing at the onset of an Assyrian conquest.

Matthew Henry's Commentary sheds light to this parallel:

"They shall be as the cities (so it may be supplied) which the Canaanites left, the old inhabitants of the land, because of the children of Israel, when God brought them in with a high hand, to take possession of that good land, cities which they built not. As the Canaanites then fled before Israel, so Israel should now flee before the Assyrians. And herein the word of God was fulfilled, that, if they committed the same abominations, the land should spue them out, as it spued out the nations that were before them" [219]

Israel's current decay was edging them closer to the point of no hope, whereas the nations of Canaan had decayed beyond hope. Canaan allowed the sun to set on their day, and with the sun's setting they removed themselves from the literal light of the sun, and the figurative light of the son of God. Entering darkness, without the lifeline of hope, had become eternal for the Canaanites who remained in the land.

Re-joining the Discussion

If you made the choice to stop for coffee and to re-join this discussion; welcome back!

God is love, and we learn God's love through one of the most famous of all scripture, a beautiful scripture; *'Love is patient ... and ... keeps no record of wrong.'* [220] The destination for this love remains directed towards every man, woman and child regardless of their ethnicity, family history or circumstance.

Yet, there are many people who subscribe to God as being a God of indiscriminate vengeance and killing. There are many who would even consider God to be an initiator of genocide. One group offers no less than 36 scriptures to defend their case that God hates children, whilst Richard Dawkins pulls no punches:

"The God of the Old Testament is arguably the most unpleasant character in all fiction: jealous and proud of it; a petty, unjust, unforgiving control-freak; a vindictive, bloodthirsty ethnic cleanser; a misogynistic, homophobic, racist, infanticidal, genocidal, filicidal, pestilential, megalomaniacal, sadomasochistic, capriciously malevolent bully." [221]

I admit to needing a dictionary to fully comprehend Dawkins level of conviction, and wonder *'how I would respond if I met Richard Dawkins to offer my defence of God'*. How would I respond? As God followers, what is our response? Is my passion as deep and convincing as Dawkins passion?

Perhaps we quietly agree with Dawkins and journey through life with an uncomfortable version of God built on misinformation and isolated opinions formed with little or no grounds of validity. We become unsure why God did what he did, but we remain thankful that the God we serve today is not the same God as the God of the Old Testament. We form opinions on the input side of the equation, and just like the missing dollar quandary, we find ourselves believing an answer that is false. Possibly, we prefer simply to ignore the hard questions of faith and live in fear of meeting an atheist or someone who is angry at God. We hide away from engaging our faith, just in case we are caught under-prepared in our defence of the gospel.

Perhaps we have a hidden and quiet fear that one day God calls us to be a missionary in some far off land as pay-back for something we may have done in the past. So it becomes more convenient to ignore God and to tune away from his voice.

The thought of outreach may have seemed inviting, and even exciting in the passion of our early Christian experience, but over time our faith developed into something more complex and technical and we no longer feel called to share God's love which is convenient, as through life's experiences, we're no longer fully confident of all the ways of God.

Or we simply ignore the Old Testament, stop at Jude and get confused with Ananias and Sapphira. We allow ourselves to become bound by the fear of being caught by some kind of shortcoming in our own personal lives. Perhaps a secret only me and God know about, and God only knows because he disturbingly knows everything, and not because we discuss it.

Wrong interpretations of God, and tainted versions of life rob us of our ability to love God and to share God's love. On the surface, subscribing to these interpretations may appear to make life less complicated, but in the long-term, they simply make our understanding and experience of life shallow and incomplete. Whilst allowing the impact of these wrong interpretations of God to take hold within society leading to communities erasing the very thought of God, and the very relevance of God. For some these wrong interpretations provide a foundation of targeted contempt towards God leading to condemning God. In many ways, it can prove easier to condemn God than to understand God.

Condemning God is usually one-dimensional, all we need is to form an opinion based on an incomplete view of God and then speak:

"Opinion is really the lowest form of human knowledge. It requires no accountability, no understanding. The highest form of knowledge ... is empathy, for it requires us to suspend our egos and live in another's world. It requires profound purpose larger than the self kind of understanding."
[222]

The challenge, however, is how the opinion is formed.

When asked *'if you have one question to ask God, what would it be,"* British comedian Stephen Fry provided the following:

"How dare you create a world in which there is such misery that is not our fault? It's not right, it's utterly, utterly evil. Why should I respect a capricious, mean-minded, stupid God that creates a world that is so full of injustice and pain?" [223]

Although this quote may seem severe, it is relevant for those who feel anger towards God and his followers.

With Canaan often being the root of anger towards God, how does this dark episode, quite possibly the most contentious sequence of Biblical text sit with the God of love who brings life and not death? If we desire an intimate relationship with God, and if we desire to receive His complete blessing and the fullness of his true love, we do need to understand the fullness of God; otherwise we run the risk of having a fear-based and incomplete interaction with God.

God always offers redemption, and scripture builds a solid foundation of God's philosophy towards redemption. We see this philosophy in the life of Noah and God's desire for pre-flood society to turn from evil and engage faith. The Canaanites and peoples of the pre-flood age share the common trait; both had become evil. Peter reveals how Noah was not simply a boat builder during the Ark's decades-long construction, rather, his primary calling was a *'preacher of righteousness'* [224]

Genesis[225] reveals the pre-flood condition of the world, where evil filled the earth and permeated the very fabric of society. Inhabitants of pre-flood society who had not fallen outside of redemption would have responded to Noahs' preaching and would have felt the increasing tugs on their heart strings.

God set the countdown to the flood at 120 years; [226] 120 years for Noah's message of righteousness to change the course of nations, and plentiful time for the process of increased warnings to fully develop. In hindsight, we can look back and wonder if Noah's century of delivering a message of righteousness really made any difference. At the close of the century, it was still only eight people who responded to salvation. Yet what this story reveals is God reaching out in unconditional love for over a century, longing that none would be lost.

Humanity dictates how our stories end. God gives warnings about coming disaster, and people respond to these warnings as they please. Eight people fled the flood, Rahab and her family fled Jericho and Lot and his family fled the destruction of Sodom and Gomorrah.

This book is firmly grounded on the conclusion that God is good, and we use the three governing metaphors ((i) Jesus, ii) God's autobiography in Exodus 34:6, and iii) Holy Spirit) to explore and investigate this claim. John 3:16 simply states that God loves the world, and he's willing to die for the world. This is a global statement, reaching every nation, tribe, every tongue, reverberating through the galaxies and projects forward and extends backwards. There is no doubt as to the intention of God's love towards Canaan. The work of the enemy is to rob us of this truth, and if he cannot rob us, he will try to make us doubt the truth.

In his book, 'Repenting of Religion', Gregory Boyd writes:

"In this fallen, Satan-oppressed world we live in, there will certainly be many occasions for us to doubt God. For this reason we must be rooted and grounded in God's love as revealed in Jesus Christ, and in nothing else." [227]

Jesus, as God on earth is remarkable in the way he lived his life. No human has ever loved like Jesus, and his message of peace and reconciliation is fault-proof. To help gain a panoramic view on God's love towards the Canaanites, we need to look no further than Jesus encountering a Canaanite woman:

"you have great faith! Your request is granted" [228]

What becomes major symbolism in this statement is how God makes no differentiation between Jew and Gentile as to who can receive his love, grace and mercy. This symbolism is forcefully elevated by choosing a Canaanite. Jesus came to earth to seek and save all who are lost; this really is the heart of God. In Mark we meet Jesus walking the streets of new Jericho offering healing to Blind Bartemius; [229] and new Jericho became the outplaying of another famous Gospel story; the calling of Zacchaeus the Tax Collector. [230]

There's no hesitation, there's no deliberation on behalf of Jesus, and there's no sense of annoyance that Canaan lived on; just a simple welcome, a loving transaction of honour, followed by a miracle of healing. This is God in relationship.

In Canaan, God didn't come with an army to destroy; this would have been the war-God, the angry-God, possibly the karma-God, instead, God came with a broken heart. Many Jews during the time of Jesus deeply desired a king to restore the earthly Jewish Kingdom, by force if necessary. By contrast, it was the passiveness of Jesus that triggered tension, resulting in anger and offence for many. It's perhaps this non-aggressive stance that led Judas to betray Jesus. In the eyes of Judas, Jesus was not playing the part of the conqueror.

Jesus, as the full representation of God on earth, became our reference point for all who God is; the unveiled view of God.

In studying the life of Jesus, there's no trace of evidence pointing to God operating out of **doubt, fear** or **entitlement**. He was resolute in his identity, he didn't fear the schemes of the enemy, and even though he was able to call on legions of angels to help in his darkest hour, he didn't claim his entitlement.

God remains forever the same, yet there's a marked difference in God's interaction with humanity between the testaments.

"There is a time for everything, and a season for every activity under the heavens" [231]

This is true for the testaments. The Old Testament highlights the fall of humanity, the separation of the First Adam, and the loss of paradise, whilst prophesying our coming Messiah. The New Testament sees the Second Adam, highlights grace, the joy of relationship, teaches life through Christ and awaits paradise restored.

Even in the apparent harshness of some Old Testament stories, God's justice always remained merciful; and is absolute in contrast to man's justice, and the devil's torture.[232]

This book does not look to hide God's actions, or to put a good spin on a bad story; rather, and like the *The Missing Dollar Riddle* this book aims to check the validity of the input.

God's view on life and death remains beyond our comprehension. Demographers expect me to live till I'm 80 years; my life is temporal – a tad shy of 30,000 sunrises. I have a sense of eternity in my heart,[233] but I have yet to experience the fullness of eternity. God sees life through this fullness of eternity – alpha and omega – without beginning and without end. When we look at death, we need to pose the question; is it a bad thing? We may be challenged with the instrument of death, yet regardless of belief or background, all cultures collectively accept death as a reality.

Whilst living in the shadows of the industrial heartland of the northeast of England where steel, ships and coal once ruled, we became good friends with Ron. Ron had a big heart and just as big a commitment to hospitality. Ron was hosting a barbeque and through a series of events, he was set alight. Ron came nervously close to death, and his testimony afterwards was one of not being fearful of death, but he didn't want death to come through the pain of fire; it hurt and it was scary and he felt too young. Ron survived and his understanding of life, death and eternity were remarkably different.

Many would see expulsion from Eden as a punishment for Adam and Eve, whereas perhaps it needs to be seen as an act of mercy. Sin had entered our experience, the whole earth groaned under this weight of sin, and biology started to degenerate. Cells started the process of malfunction, and the gene-pool was negatively impacted. We literally started to die, and this was a new experience. Death had entered our realm yet the mechanism of death would also provide the escape from suffering.

Genesis introduces two specific trees in Eden:

1) The Tree of the Knowledge of Good and Evil, and
2) The Tree of Life

Chapter 26
The Knowledge of Evil, and Leaving Eden

"Whenever you see confusion, you can be sure that something is wrong. Disorder in the world implies that something is out of place. Usually, at the heart of all disorder you will find man in rebellion against God. It began in the Garden of Eden and continues to this day."

– A. W. Tozer [234]

The impact of sin is that we became exposed to the knowledge of evil. We began to understand evil without the self-capacity to withstand evil. Although we were made in the image of God, we were not designed with a mechanism to shield us from exposure to evil. At this point everything changed for humanity, we became vulnerable and needy. Yet, nothing changed for God. Adam and Eve were removed from Paradise and continued the human species, passing on from one generation to the next this exposure to evil; yet adaptation of our species over the years could never develop an antidote for the effects of evil. Evil killed us, and Jesus saves us.

The Eden rebellion established a beach-head for the kingdom of Darkness. In the 21st Century, this dark-Kingdom develops through war, slavery, illness, suffering and robs us of our most basic human need: the fullness of relationship with Abba. By robbing this human need, our identity searches for an elusive anchor and soon we become prisoners of our own fake identities, replacing confidence with statements similar to: *"I don't believe in God"*, *"I don't need God"* or *"All gods are the same, it really doesn't matter which one you believe in."*

Deep down the human race seeks answers, seeks to belong, and desires to know where we fit, and who we are. Regardless of faith, we intrinsically sense something is out there, where there's more to life than the natural eye can see. I'd hedge a bet that life's defining questions are questions of identity:

- Who am I?
- Where am I from?
- Why am I here?
- What can I do?
- Where am I going?

When we fail to find God we'll continue searching for answers with no hope for fulfilment. We develop a false sense of identity often resulting in harm to others; this is the challenge of navigating free-will outside of pure love.

In the early stages of writing this book, flight MH17 had been shot down over Ukraine and my attention turned to newsfeeds,

"...closer up burning wreckage and other charred fragments ... have turned these Ukrainian fields into a scene from hell. [Helen Dafedjaiye and Tessa Wong concluded with the question] So how on earth could this have happened." [235]

"How on earth could this have happened" is a sobering question needing to be asked in the wider context of the clash of kingdoms. At the point of rebellion, the spiritual battle hit earth and human relations became scarred by tension. Unfortunately, this tension spilt to the physical.

People hurt people; school-yard name calling to international warfare. The question of *'why people suffer'* perhaps needs to be asked in the wider context of *'why people make other people suffer?'*

The use of *terror* and *evil* are common when reporting on news. Most people agree with these usages especially if describing crimes targeting children and the vulnerable; whilst falling short in acknowledging the destructive allure of the Kingdom of Darkness as the originator, promoter, and source of this evil. Instead, finding blame for evil contained within the complexity of the human frame.

Eating from the *Tree of the knowledge of Good and Evil* resulted in death and expulsion from Eden. If we'd then eaten from the *Tree of Life* we would have gained eternal life within the context of our dying bodies; being expelled from Eden removed the opportunity to eat from the Tree of Life.

It's hard to imagine eternity living in a body riddled with pain, disease and torment without any hope of death. Genesis sheds light on this eventuality:

"And the Lord God said, "The man has now become like one of us, knowing good and evil. He must not be allowed to reach out his hand and take also from the tree of life and eat, and live forever." [236]

Eating from the *Tree of Life* would have resulted in an eternity spent on a death-bed gasping our last breath, but our last breath never coming. An utterly awful experience – the world plagued by the living dead with no hope of escape. Revelation gives a glimpse of life where death had temporarily been removed from the human existence:

"During those days people will seek death but will not find it; they will long to die, but death will elude them." [237]

Death was to be our exit from pain, and eternal life was to be received through death. The Bible narrative gives many examples and pictures of this concept:

- The seed that falls to the ground [238]
- Jonah in the Whale [239]
- Noah in his ark [240]

Life had become hard and we suffered an allergic reaction to sin, but mercy ensured our suffering would be temporary.

Many nations struggle with the question *'how to deal with an ageing population'*. It's a good question needing a good answer and we need to care and provide for our ageing populations. But can you envisage a scenario where this ageing population never died? Of an existence where incurable sickness continued its degenerative march but stopped just short of the threshold of death?

Although pain and suffering are far from being light-hearted, I raised a chuckle from the TV listings a few nights ago. Dr Who was playing, and the write-up for *"The Doctor Dances"*[241] offered the following enlightenment,

> *"A zombie army is on the march as plague sweeps through wartime London"*

Can you imagine an existence without the freedom of death? Where the most evil people in the history of humanity were alive and active, similar to the catch-phrase from the Roly-Poly toys *"Weebles wobble, but they don't fall down"*; you can knock them down, but they'll keep on getting back up. This statement from Dr Who describes such a future: *'zombie'*, *'army'*, *'plague'*, and *'war'*.

I grew up in England during the 70s and 80s and became part of the *'scared-generation'*; a generation of kids subjected to Dr Who, who learned the art of *'hiding behind the sofa every Saturday night'*. Dr Who is by-and-large a quirky quintessential British drama. By 1963 Daleks arrived and were beaming into living rooms the length and breadth of the nation ensuring Saturday evenings would never be the same again.

Daleks were a fascinating race of mutant cyborgs from the planet Skaro with a long history of war pitted against the Thals. Towards the end of this millennial-war, Davros genetically modified the Dals creating the Daleks with the inability to feel any sense of remorse, empathy, or compassion. He did, however, leave the Dalek with one surviving emotion; hatred.

A deadly race of cyborgs void of any emotion besides hatred became a powerful tool in Davros' vision of universal domination and the purging of any non-Dalek life. Without a saviour, humanity would be doomed. One lone defender, a Time-Lord, simply known as The Dr rose to take a stand.

Daleks have become a national legacy, yet they were silly things; a robotic shell with horrendous vision making escape easy by standing behind them, or to cover their one eyepiece, sending the Dalek into a panicked frenzy.

If you're confused by Daleks, chances are you're not British. But if you've seen children running around in a state of frenzy declaring 'Exterminate! Exterminate!' in a deep robotic style voice chances are they are playing Daleks. Daleks are entrenched in British culture. Politicians have used the term to describe opponents, Daleks have featured on the front of British postage stamps, Daleks have met the British Royal Family and in 2013 Prince Charles famously interpreted a Dalek. Daleks have found inclusion in the Oxford English Dictionary, and in 2008 it was reported that nine out of ten British children could correctly identify a Dalek.[242] That's nine out of ten; 90%, and in the same survey less than 33% could identify a Magpie; a very common British bird.

Daleks are killing machines birthed out of war. Their actual creator, Kim Nation, developed the concept of the Dalek through his personal experience of German bombings and the rise of the Nazis. Dalek's were authoritarian and they ruthlessly pursued absolute conformity and conquest.

Looking back, and re-visiting some of the more frightening years of my childhood, I do find it hard to believe Dr Who was originally aired by the BBC as a children's educational programme.[243] Regardless of its educational credentials, the show can leave a profound thought. What would life be like if hatred was the only emotion? I wonder how close this scenario is to the reality of an eternity without God.

God is a pursuer, and the Bible in its entirety is the greatest romance ever told; the world's greatest love-story, of God pursuing humanity through every page, through every story, every comma and through every full-stop. We, his beloved, reject his love time and time again and prostitute ourselves with a whole host of temptations. We ignore God, get angry with God, turn our backs on him, chase alternative lovers, generally ignore God and then blame God for the mess we've made. Yet God remains relentless in his pursuit of us. This is love, and it's only through God's relentless pursuit that we're provided with the framework of life.

Eternity cannot go on as an endless pursuit, however. At the end of the day, this becomes tiring. There needs to be a time where the lover ends his pursuit and we enjoy his love, where perfect unity commences for eternity. It would not be fair to God to have him pursue for eternity, and it would not be fair on us to be pursued without the promise of absolute belonging. For those who despise God, it's perhaps not fair for them to be constantly pursued by a lover they've rejected.

God will collect his own, and we will then move to the next stage of eternity. For those not collected, the pursuit will be over. Love will be gone, and eternity will start in a sphere where the devil has dominion. Like the Daleks, hatred will rule, but unlike the Daleks there will be no Dr Who to provide redemption. This is a frightening existence, and an existence I consider is close to the reality of Canaan at the end of God's exhaustive attempts over centuries to woo them away from death.

At the end of the day people do die, we all die, even God died on the cross. Death is part of our cycle, and death is our only escape. The controversial question of death, particularly in the Old Testament relating to the reputation of God, is perhaps more to do with the event of death, rather than death itself.

Sin required death, and Jesus paid the ultimate ransom price through the giving of his life. I enjoy life, I want to live till I'm old, I want to see my sons grow to adults, to fall in love, to marry and have children. I want to enjoy travel, meet new people, see new places, yet I'm not afraid of death. But like my friend Ron, I hope it comes quickly and I hope it's still a long time off. Yet the eternity placed in my heart gives me full assurance and confidence that death is just the gateway to eternity with God in paradise restored.

The word *'good'* dominates the creation story of Genesis. Good is all we knew until the fall, then *'bad'* was introduced to our narrative. Sin required death and sin brought death, whilst God brings life.

By developing an understanding that without God our default position is death, we move from a position of blaming God for death to thanking God for life. However, we can assume a position of non-thankfulness and unbelief in God, yet God continues pursuing us in hope of relationship restored.

In many ways, this can be seen as God having us on life-support, where we retain the freedom to jump down from the bed, and disconnect the tubes. God could have locked the clinic door, positioned guards at the entrance and chained us to the bed; but this wouldn't be love. This would be removing our freedom and holding us captive against our wishes, thus removing the bastion of human rights and free will, captured beautifully by C. S. Lewis:

"He wants them to learn to walk and must therefore take away His hand" [244]

By carrying a narrative of God's judgment and God's anger, we're speaking from a limited understanding of the message of the Bible.

In his 1986 hit, *"You Can Call me Al,"*[245] Paul Simon introduces us to Al who ponders the reality of navigating a harsh world through the softness of a fragile heart; this is a profound concept. Simon penned this song whilst reflecting on his time in South Africa during the apartheid years. Simon was confronted with the cruel system of apartheid and searched for meaning and words to fully describe this reality.

Growing up I used to think apartheid segregation was based on two groups: blacks and whites; it was after spending a year in South Africa I learned the system to be more sinister than my simple understanding. Government officials used a cruel rudimentary classification system based on physical appearance and features that would, in some cases result in members of the same family receiving different classifications. Four main groups had been established (Black, White, Indian, and Coloured) and within these four groups were a number of sub-groups allowing some people re-categorised as *'honorary whites'*. This was cruelty, and as humans, we needed to confront this, and in considering this cruelty, many questions were raised.

The Bible hints at the Government of Heaven,[246] a government based on relationship with perfect unity between father, son and spirit; a government where love, purpose and identity are complete and perfect. The purpose of Heaven's government is relationship. When the principles of heaven's government are reflected on earth, the community is developed and strengthened. Without heaven's dynamic, world governments operate on a continuum of achieving good results through to delivering harsh systems of control. To make matters worse our adversary, the devil, is intent on manipulating governments and regimes to operate from his set of values; death, destruction and pain, and greed, self-sufficiency and independence.

I consider there's a point where earthly governments become so intent on hatred they open themselves to the dreadful spectre of the devil's influence; the Third Reich, Canaan, the Khmer Rouge, and the National Party of South Africa's apartheid to a name a few. History shows these governments had a strong ideology, but poor values. In the case of apartheid, mankind developed the government that created the policies that established apartheid, and once the kindling was burning the devil fanned these flames with hatred until the whole nation started to burn.

Through the song *"You can call me Al"* Paul Simon invites us to join his struggle of the challenge of having a soft heart in a harsh environment. Simon needed an outlet to describe the context of his observations, of a soft heart encountering a cruel world.

As Jesus-followers we observe the context of a hurting world and speak into this hurt through the median of love and the vehicle of our talents and abilities. The reason we have soft hearts is because God has a soft-heart. The reason our soft-hearts break is because we're birthed from the identity of God. The testimony of our soft-hearts breaking at the struggle of humanity is compelling evidence that God's soft-heart breaks and he feels the pain of our hurting world.

A recent article I read *"Not in the mood for love"* brought some light-hearted comic relief to my commute home, and raised a series of questions:

> *"if it seems you are permanently single while everyone else around you is in a relationship, blame your DNA. Scientists have identified a "singleton gene.""* [247]

During God's assessment of creation he declared with abounding joy and enthusiasm *'our DNA is very good'*. Our DNA has degenerated from this original state-of-perfection, however, and to explain social disconnectedness and the struggle of life through DNA-degeneration removes eternal hope, and excuses the work of the devil. A dangerous conclusion is reached where identities are formed through an involuntary process. How would we explain the existence of evil? The existence of evil is real and originates from the spiritual realm.

The answer to *'why people suffer'* or *'why people allow people to suffer'* is rooted in attempts of the Dark-Kingdom to establish values and principles directly opposing life. Any explanation for human suffering void of a spiritual reality acts as a blinker to the reality of life.

Thankfully evil has been defeated, and its days are numbered; the Dark-Kingdom is a failed kingdom living on the dying fumes of its existence. Jesus won our victory and we share in this victory. Jesus-believers have the legal right to oppose the work of the devil and the legal power to thwart its final attempts at defeating God's children through false identity.

We are human. We have a mind, body and soul. We think. We process. We get hurt, and we make decisions. We analyse and we have a general aversion to risk.

We can travel through life with hard heads attempting to navigate challenging contexts, equipped with soft hearts looking for belonging. As humans, we have intelligence and we desire to understand the context of our existence.

So much of our existence, however, remains shrouded in the context of mystery, made all the worse by an antagonist relentless in the art of deception. It's perhaps little wonder why people struggle through life. Unfortunately, the devil deceives well and often leaves the victim unaware of being deceived, and we're left to navigate a confusing life grappling with questions similar to:

- Is there a God?
- If there is a God why is there pain?
- Why do followers of one God go to war with the followers of another God?
- Are the gods not strong enough to fight it out themselves?
- If there isn't a God, what I am doing here?
- Is life all about me, and my pursuit of happiness?
- Has evolution provided me with a body to exist within, yet has offered no comfort or answer for the internal yearning of my heart?

When our view of God is veiled we fail to see clearly and soon become disabled through navigating a hard world with a soft heart; feeling let down by God who seems to operate from judgment and anger.

The devil will do anything in his power to destroy God's reputation. He'll use stories from the Bible, stories from our own lives, and fabricated stories to distract us. He'll encourage us to ponder Canaan through the filter of revenge and vindictiveness. He'll place questions in our minds as to the finer details of the Law of Moses and challenge us to question God's motives and accuse God of being a stringent, vindictive and controlling God. Yet, just as we have discussed the conquest of Canaan, where by now, I hope we can see the conquest through the tears of pain shed by a broken-hearted God; we'll pause for a moment and consider the need for God's direct intervention through the giving of the Law, or the need of a fence to guide us, where for much of the context of the Old Testament, society lived in spiritual darkness desperately needing Jesus to come and bring forth light.

Chapter 27
The Fence

"It will never happen to me."

– Captain EJ Smith (Captain of the Titanic) [248]

Within Eden, we had the parameters of the Garden, and after the fall, Adam and Eve were driven from the Garden into a hostile environment. They had left the safety of Eden behind. To assist the furtherance of humanity, new parameters were developed, eventually leading to a set of written Laws given by Moses. Unfortunately for humanity, our forefathers shied away from full dependency on God and requested human advocates to stand before God on their behalf. Moses became an advocate between God and humanity, and it was Moses who introduced the Law. This Law of Moses would have to suffice.

At Eden, we learned nomadic wandering. Yet we were never left alone. The face-to-face intimate relationship with God had become a distant notion, to be fully restored in the future, yet remained shrouded in mystery. We were now beyond paradise and evil had infiltrated the landscape where ethical, spiritual and moral decision-making became confused. We were prone to stray and prone to competition. In love, God provided a safeguard, a fence to allow freedom within security.

A good friend teaches on the attributes of God, and once shared a simple yet stirring analogy of creation spoilt. I've taken the liberty to add greatly to this analogy. Through this analogy, look for God's unconditional love, our rebellion, and the need for a fence.

Suppose da Vinci created a perfect oil canvas and constructed a perfect gallery to reveal his masterpiece. Desiring others to share his creation, da Vinci opened the gallery doors and welcomed people with unhindered access to his work. A pot containing thick black oil was mysteriously placed beside the painting with a simple sign, 'do not touch'. It wasn't long until peoples' interest in this mysterious pot of mesmerising liquid grew.

Every day da Vinci would walk through his gallery, celebrating his creation with all who'd come to see. As days turned to weeks, weeks to months, and months turning to seasons, peoples' adoration for da Vinci and his creation waned. As much as their interest waned, their interest in the pot of oil began to grow over time. What was this mysterious liquid? Is it calling from the deep? We do need to find out.

Then one dreadful day, the urge to discover the mystery substance became too much. It now became their lives ambition to solve this mystery.

The oil was thick, and it was fun, providing an unexplored sensation to their finger-tips. This stuff was good, and peoples' minds exploded with scenarios and dreams of how they could use this mysterious element. A voice cried out, *'it needs to be free, let it loose'*. *'It needs to be experienced by all'*. *'I know'*, shouted a different voice, *'let's add it to da Vinci's canvas'*.

A momentary silence ensued, giving a brief time for recollection, but not enough time to fully consider their plan. *'Let's do this thing'*. Hands reached for the pot and with one collective movement, and with pride desperately seeking to enter their hearts, thick black oil was released from the pot, flew through the environment, and embellished the canvas. Darkness covered the canvas and somehow this strange darkness seemed to have filled their hearts and soul. Although they looked the same, the people felt different about each other and not only different from each other, they began to feel different themselves. There was no oil on their hearts, but they felt dirty, even ashamed.

But, da Vinci, although unnoticed, remained present all along. His heart was torn but his love was secure. This strange sense of hurt and love would see da Vinci rip apart the canvas from another of his creations to help bring comfort and to wipe away the oil from their hands. The creation was ruined, stained and by now was obscure, and returning the canvas to its former glory was no longer an option.

Someone obviously left the pot. They're the ones to blame. Why would someone even leave the pot where it was? Could it have been da Vinci? Had da Vinci left the pot? Why didn't the pot have a lid, a locked lid? Of all the stars in the night sky, why oh why, did it get put here?

The people quickly walked off, surprisingly showing little remorse; instead engaging the game of blaming each other whilst questioning the sanity of da Vinci for leaving an open pot of dirty oil in the gallery. It wasn't their fault.

The masterpiece remained in place, but mystery surrounded the work. The full picture was shrouded, veiled. Within no time, da Vinci revealed his plan to set everything right. He raised guides and experts to teach and help uncover the mystery. Over the years many of these guides were beaten, ridiculed, simply ignored and even killed.[249] There were times, however, when their authority on the artwork was valued and people listened.[250] Yet there were dark periods also, times when it seemed the artwork had simply vanished from collective conscious. During times of war, the painting was looted and destroyed further.

Many artists rose up in this vacuum and presented their pieces of work, but viewing their work came at a devastating cost.

da Vinci had a plan, however. His canvas was beautiful, yet despite this beauty, his heart was bursting with love for the villains of the story. da Vinci had the plan to reach out to them and he stuck to his plan, ultimately costing him his life to make the painting available for all the world to see.

As with God, da Vinci reached out to the perpetrators of the crime and engaged them through relationship offering an immediate way back. God forgave, but in wisdom, realised a code was needed to help navigate moral, ethical and spiritual decisions. After witnessing rebellion, he concluded the need for a framework – a fence – to separate evil influences from the pride of his creation; me and you.

Recently I was driving interstate. Whilst driving through the night it struck me how the headlights only extended 100 metres and beyond the reach of the headlights was darkness; to the left darkness, to the right darkness, and behind, darkness. Yet, I had complete confidence in the condition of the road, how there would be no sharp corners or virtually any corner without road signs guiding me. You see, the State Government has a track record of delivering and maintaining excellent roads, and besides the threat of wildlife at dusk, there really was no other threat. I could tune into local radio and get regular condition updates. This combined track record of delivery and confidence in the environment allowed me to travel into sheer darkness at 100km per hour in a landscape I was not familiar with. I needed to stay alert and in tune to the environment, yet I had confidence in the road. The road provided safety, security and a means to get to my destination. I had the freedom to go off-road, but I really wouldn't have lasted that long, the car wasn't built for those conditions and I would soon end up lost, in danger, and in need of assistance.

In this instance, I'm glad for the imaginary fence the road provided, glad the roads were maintained, and grateful my vehicle had safety features. We can look back on the Law of Moses and see a strict totalitarian God, or we can look back on the Law of Moses and see that it was needed to establish a smooth road to our destination; Jesus Christ. The Law of Moses was not a tool for God to bring judgment; it was a necessary system to protect humanity.

UN Peacekeepers, in a vague sense, can provide some insight into the role of the Law of Moses. The Law of Moses provided safe passage and safe-havens for people to live within, and just as United Nations Peacekeepers are limited in their scope, and operate out of pre-defined limits, the Law also had a limited scope.

For refugees and the internally displaced, safe passages and safe-zones are mere shadows of how they desire to live. My family and a group of students recently spent time on Lesvos, a Greek island just off the coast of Turkey, responding to the humanitarian refugee crisis. Each day we would receive countless refugees at all times of the day and night; thousands of mothers with small children would arrive and often be soaked to the skin with sea water. The temperature was cold, and we often experienced strong winds, snow and rain. Although these refugees were grateful to have made it to Lesvos, they were none the less part of a system. Being in Europe, the fear of rape, torture and death may have dissipated, but you could see in their eyes that they were barely existing in a shadow of how they wanted to live, and how they desired to raise their children.

The Law was a mere shadow of how God wanted us to live. Under the Law, protection was available, but when people strayed from the safe parameters, protection was no longer guaranteed. The nations of Canaan walked away from God's love, and we too can walk away from God's love, and make life choices that plot a course running contrary to God. In this instance, and similar to the Canaanites, we walk within the reach of the devil's leash and subject ourselves to the influence of the devil.

In many ways, we're like Lemmings from the classic 1990s video game, and just like Lemmings we needed help with barriers and bridges. We desperately needed a redeemer, and a desperate price was set; the blood of the redeemer's son.

We are all great people with amazing potential, nevertheless, our bad habits get us into trouble and when we let bad habits rule our lives we leave ourselves open for the enemy. If done in isolation, a bad habit impacts the individual; when the individual is part of a family the family is impacted. When this family is part of a community, then society is impacted. When many communities form bad habits, whole nations can be impacted.

God has provided an amazing life with opportunities beyond measure. We've been given the keys to this kingdom, and we're encouraged to have a whole load of fun; within parameters. Luke writes:

"For in him we live and move and have our being" [251]

If we demand our own rights and develop our own system of navigating we not only risk getting in trouble ourselves but also endanger others and take away from their freedom.

God offers freedom yet on so many occasions we ignore freedom and pursue rights. Until we reach a position of confidence in giving up our rights and choosing freedom we will constantly battle the concept of God, battle the rightful ownership of our lives and the world, and miss the fullness of our temporary existence on God's creation.

Relationship is the underlying message of the Bible and humanity was created out of the desire for relationship. One of the early observable signs of the fall in Genesis is how the relationship between man and woman became strained and the relationship between humankind and God became confused. As this relational gap deepened and became more complex, we learned new ways to deal with the emotions we were never created to cope with (greed, lust, power, insecurity, pain, failure and hurt to name a few) and the physical actions that these emotions led to (break-up, anxiety, violence, and divorce). Rarely can these emotions and actions be isolated to the experience of a single human; inevitably they will impact partners, children, family and friends. When these emotions and actions are brought into the fabric of society, the results have increasing ramifications for communities, and nations.

I consider this to be the case with the nations of Canaan. They'd abandoned their inheritance as people loved by God and chose a different path ultimately leading to destruction. Yet, their decisions on how to conduct and organise themselves and how they would shape society were not just formed from redeemable bad habits, they were catastrophic actions, resulting in untold suffering and evil.

Earlier we discussed the simple equation of determining if something is of God or not. Simply put:

- God is good and the devil is bad
- God brings life and the devil brings death
- God is truth and the devil is the father of lies

The Canaanites had been mastered by the bringer of death.

God in human form, Jesus, wept over the state of Jerusalem. As we read the context of Jesus' tears over Jerusalem, ponder the similarities of the fall of Jerusalem and the fall of Jericho:

"As he approached Jerusalem and saw the city, he wept over it and said, "If you, even you, had only known on this day what would bring you peace—but now it is hidden from your eyes. The days will come upon you when your enemies will build an embankment against you and encircle you and hem you in on every side. They will dash you to the ground, you and the children within your walls.

They will not leave one stone on another, because you did not recognize the time of God's coming to you." [252]

This passage lays all the blame of impending destruction at the hands of humanity. In this picture God is a grieving observer, yet an observer who would pay for their salvation with his very life. This prophecy eventuated in AD70 during the first Roman-Jewish War, approximately 1 million[253] were killed in the carnage, and Jerusalem and its temple fell to Titus.

God wept over Jerusalem, and God wept over Jericho. Joshua and his army stood on the precipice of conquest and were soon to become men-of-war. God stood on the banks of the river as a broken-hearted Father. In the same way, God weeps over each situation that robs us of identity and steals our purpose.

Chapter 28
The Broken Heart of God

"A broken heart bleeds tears."

- Steve Maraboli [254]

We catch glimpses of the heart of God in the parable of the prodigal son with all types of vice becoming secondary to the love relationship between father and son. The son, in disregarding his rightful position squanders his inheritance and enters a life of sin. We meet the son at a juncture prior to his return, in a pig pen.

This picture would have unnerved Jewish listeners, and I wonder if they waited with baited breath for the outcome. With pigs being deemed amongst the most unclean of all living animals, and with a son bringing dishonour to his father and hiring himself into servitude, how would the story end? It ends with a pure demonstration of Exodus 34:6; the pure love of God who looked beyond the swine-pen, to see the heart of his lost son. Redemption was available to Rahab, just as redemption was sought for the son. This is the love of God.

Jesus surrounded himself with prostitutes, tax collectors and others referred collectively as '*sinners.*' God's love is not selective. I'm challenged with the concept of salvation being only for those who God foreknew would respond to his love. Corinthians[255] lays out a written tapestry of God's love. Peter writes[256] that God desires none would perish, that all would come to repentance. The evidence of God's love stacks up convincingly.

Life can be cruel. I remember visiting a war-torn society several years back and learning from community development workers how children were enlisted to the national army. The children were fed a toxic mix of drugs and once '*high*', the children were given a machine gun and ordered to rape a woman. The woman was brutalised and the child would never be the same again. They had lost their innocence, they had disgraced themselves, and they had become addicted to a drug. The army now had a soldier.

If we associate suffering as coming from God, we confuse the author of life with the bringer of death. We become confused, disillusioned and start accusing God. The devil is subtle, knowing a full assault, for a third time is futile. It seems, for now, the devil enjoys a level of success through influencing our minds and disturbing our framework of understanding with subtle questions, and dropping seeds of doubt; covering our eyes with a veil:

- If God is a loving God, why does he send people to hell?
- Why does God call us to act justly whilst he has the freedom to act unjustly?

We take on an accuser's mindset, and our agenda becomes contrary to freedom. We reject the realities of life and speak the narrative of the devil's propaganda.

I do believe that God, who brings life, is able to sustain life. I do not think it any matter of concern to God that the earth's population has reached seven billion. Yet, I do think he's grieved at the way we manage resources, is heartbroken at the way some of us treat other humans and is disappointed at the way the majority remains silent whilst the minority victimise and brutalise those whom God loves.

It can be easy to allow opinion, personal experience, and tradition to block our view of the simple truth of God's love, and we need to remain focused on what is incontrovertibly true.

If we read accounts of the actions of God and these actions seem to run contrary to God's character chances are we're reading the conclusion, and end result. It's as though we've entered a courtroom on the final day during prosecutions' well-rehearsed, informed and convincing final deliberation. What we've missed, however, is the whole case. Reading the final act of

God can be similar, where we've missed the process of increasing opportunities to turn to God, the increasing warnings that our life choices are leading to destruction and increasing sanctions which act as timely reminders to recalibrate ourselves.

In studying human development it's generally acknowledged and agreed that there has to be varying degrees of consequences to teach right from wrong. The body is not designed to carry sin, and although sin at first may seem sweet, the soul soon determines its negative impact and will give increasing warnings about sins presence. We have a conscience and whilst our heart beats, our conscience will act as our moral guide; our internal warning system.

Chapter 29
Carriers of God's Character

"Aslan: You doubt your value. Don't run from who you are."

- C.S. Lewis, *Prince Caspian* [257]

We are made in God's perfect image. Yet in the fall we started to question our identity and initiated the internal and ongoing battle within our souls as we struggle for identity. Walking in true identity is important, and to gain true identity we need complete confidence in God's reputation, in Father who gives our identity.

We've had the knowledge of good and evil since the fall at Eden and we are no longer ignorant to evil and injustice; we know injustice through the remnant of justice deposited in our hearts. We see the news and instinctively know when wrong has been achieved, this is because the presence of evil runs contrary to our conscience and our conscience was not designed to cope with, and to handle evil. Micah[258] calls us to do justice and love kindness. This is possible.

At the national level, a judicial system is paramount to national success. When new countries are established a fair and functional justice system becomes an integral foundation in nation building. I witnessed the importance of this after meeting a South American lawmaker in an East Timor café shortly after independence; this lawmaker had been commissioned by the new government to establish a judicial system as a national priority.

When nations lack the power or appear unwilling to administer justice, the International Criminal Court may be engaged to intervene and make far-reaching calls for justice. Whether these national and international judicial systems work, or not, they do remain a testament to the remnant of justice deposited in our hearts. Humanity seeks justice and we become offended when we suffer injustice. Referees understand this concept. Should they make a controversial call on the field, or miss a blatant foul, they have thousands of spectators instantly reacting. 'Come on, that's not fair!'. 'Are you blind!'. 'Referee!'

Justice is part of our DNA, yet God goes beyond justice. The popular English phrase *"you can't have your cake and eat it"* suggests a person cannot eat their cake and keep the same cake, or simply put, a person is not entitled to more than they deserve.

The cupcake offers a great example of justice, mercy and grace with justice being the cake, mercy being the icing and grace being the cherry on top. If justice is what we deserve, mercy removes the punishment and grace becomes an abundant blessing. Joel captures this concept beautifully:

"Return to the Lord your God, for he is gracious and compassionate, slow to anger and abounding in love, and he relents from sending calamity. Who knows? He may turn and relent and leave behind a blessing" [259]

Preceding this verse, we learn Judah was besieged by a massive locust plague and devastating drought. Judah had turned from God and God was holding back death. Enough death, however, was filtering through to fully convince Judah of their immediate danger and of the horrors of life without God. God's heart was to bless them and to receive this blessing they needed only turn back to God.

Chapter 30
Appropriation

"In the law of debtor and creditor, appropriation of payments is the application of a particular payment for the purpose of paying a particular debt."

- Dr Bhatia, *Textbook on Legal Language and Legal Writing* [260]

Appropriation is a powerful word in the context of our redemption and liberation.

Appropriation happened at the transaction of the cross, where a price had been set and agreed upon for our liberation from the slave-market. The price was paid and legal ownership of humanity returned to God.[261] Yet, unlike traditional slave-transactions, we were not sold from one slave-master to be carried off by another slave-master. In this transaction we were given the freedom of choice; to return to our current slave-master or to choose freedom in Jesus.

Left to our own devices, humans are powerless to broker freedom from our spiritual enemy. There's nothing we can do to free ourselves, we were doomed and enslaved.

It can be hard to fully comprehend all that Jesus did at the cross and the perfection of redemption.

Yet, suppose a nation's most notorious criminal appears before the nation's most senior judge and through executive judicial power the judge grants pardon, the court would be left astounded. The judge takes this further, however, by saying, '*I understand your situation, I'm giving you free access to the nation's top private medical clinics and elite educators who will help you improve, and I will cover the expense*'; leaving the nation in an uproar. For the nation's most senior Judge to go further '*you need a family, you need love and purpose, I've already arranged the paperwork, I'd like to invite you to be my son – to share in my family's wealth and to take your place at our family table whilst receiving my full legacy. Yet, your crime cannot go unpunished. I've spoken to my only son and he is willing to stand in your place, and to receive your punishment'*; would leave the world speechless.

This is what happened at Calvary. The legal ownership of humanity's sin changed hands from the devil to God. The devil used this sin to weigh us down for eternity but God took our sin and broke its hold on us.

This is the true reputation of God; abounding grace. Amazing grace. Providing you and me with the most secure foundation to attain confidence in our identities as sons and daughters of the God of love.

The appropriation made for us at the cross saw the provision for every sin removed, and though we retain the memory of sin (partly as a remembrance of God's goodness and as the foundation of our testimony) we're liberated at the spiritual level. Often our life choices do catch-up on us, impacting our ongoing physical freedom to varying degrees, but spiritually we are free. The price for freedom was set, and paid; liberating our past, giving hope for the present, and securing our future.

I sometimes wonder if I fully understand the value of my life. For the devil, he required the ultimate price for my freedom. For God, he willingly paid this ultimate price for me; the most expensive, the most unfair and the most one-sided transaction of all time; the blood of God for a dirty rag like me.

I envision how the world would look if we collectively believed this, if our collective conscience spoke out against human exploitation.

In 1984 two influencers of British music, Bob Geldof and Midge Ure penned a song changing the public response to suffering. On 23rd October 1984 Michael Duncan Buerk had reported on the Ethiopian Famine, and suffering had been introduced to the British living-room in techno-colour. In God's plan, these were images that should never have happened.

As an impressionable teenager this song and those images made an impact, and only seeing the need for change and not the politics and economics of famine, something stirred within me. My next door neighbour Graham and I held a yard sale for Oxfam, by selling our favourite toys the local paper reported our grand total of $5.32. Perhaps a little disappointed at the grand total, nonetheless, I consider something was birthed that day helping to shape my life. Since '96 my wife and I have worked as full-time volunteers for several charities in Africa, and Asia, and it was during our time in Africa I encountered one of my most challenging experiences; witnessing suffering without the ability to help.

We were serving a medical mission where world-class teams of surgeons, nurses and medical technicians were to provide thousands of free life-changing and life-saving surgical procedures over a four-month period. Large scale screening-days were arranged in stadiums, and for many months beforehand national media had been informing the public about these screenings.

My role was to help with security and crowd control. The queue to the stadium was long, the heat was relentless and due to security concerns we could only let twenty people through to triage at a time.

I was a young naive white English man, unable to speak the local language, ignorant of local culture and had no way to comprehend the desperation of the people in the queue; many travelling days to be there. You see, in the poorest nations on earth, access to health care is almost non-existent for the masses, with poverty, security, politics and geography excluding many from the most basic of health care.

My instruction for the day seemed simple; 'only let twenty people through at a time, then close the gate and wait for instruction for the next twenty'. Logically I understood the instruction, but in my heart, I was broken. As the minutes of the day ticked, and the shadows increased, as the surgical slots were filling, the queue still snaked around the stadium. Not all would make it. How do I deal with the knowledge that once the gate is closed for the final time, I would be there closing it, and it would remain closed? Triage tents would be packed down, water stations would be removed, the fleet of vehicles would rumble home, and within a few short hours, all that would remain at the stadium is the sense of hope for some and the sense of despair for others.

I then reflected on the broken heart of God, wondering how he sees humanity with countless millions caught in cycles of poverty, millions born under oppressive regimes, many harming each other, some harming themselves, whilst a majority turn a blind-eye. And I wondered if this is the fullness of all that was given to us at the cross.

I allow myself to believe that appropriation made 2,000 years ago is valid today. When we find a way to walk in the fullness of Jesus' sacrifice and redemption, and to realise we have a living inheritance and eternal hope, then I dare to believe there is hope beyond suffering. Geldof and Ure's *"Do they know it's Christmas Time,"* speaks of a wonderful spiritual truth of how shade cannot remain in the presence of light. John captures this spiritual truth by recounting a time where Jesus addressed a crowd about his purpose on earth:

"I am the light of the world. Whoever follows me will never walk in darkness, but will have the light of life."

I look at the impact of Geldof and Ure, the Band Aid legacy, and I take delight in their achievements. Millions of pounds raised, the political agenda impacted, and providing Bono with increased volume as he continued to advocate for freedom. If the global church were to mobilise in their identity as advocates for freedom, the earth would be different:

"Very truly I tell you, whoever believes in me will do the works I have been doing, and they will do even greater things than these, because I am going to the Father".[264]

Jesus healed the sick, raised the dead, and crossed all kinds of social and cultural barriers to bring a message of love and hope.

We need to go beyond an academic understanding of suffering, and add volume to the debate, we need to engage the spiritual reality of suffering, and become the world advocators and changers we're called to be. There's nothing more God needs to do to stop suffering. For a reason beyond logic, God has called you and me to be his hands and his feet on this planet, and to be the empowered carriers of his love, his mercy and his compassion. There's nothing more God needs to do, but there's everything more we can do.

If justice is what we deserve, God's mercy provides freedom. Beyond freedom comes grace, elevating us to a position of abundant living.

Beyond the simplicity of relationship, our identity and purpose were to echo heaven and to join with the elders by declaring *'holy, holy, holy.'* [265] Instead, we doubted, questioned and took on the personality of evil, unleashing the most deadly and corrupting presence of fallen angles, leading to fallen humanity inheriting the characteristics of the fallen one. Instead of outwardly declaring *'holy, holy, holy'* from the fullness of identity, we focus inward and murmur a narrative of **fear**, **doubt** and **entitlement** creating a position of insecurity.

Chapter 31
The Renewing of the Mind

"What comes into our minds when we think about God is the most important thing about us."

– A. W. Tozer [266]

Over recent years I've been blessed to walk alongside many students on a number of discipleship schools. During the students' orientation, we participate in 'Welcome to Country'; a protocol showing respect to the traditional custodians on whose land we study, grow and are transformed.

For several years we've been honoured and blessed by having Mark, an Aboriginal elder, lead us through this protocol of welcoming the students to their land; the Wurundjeri land of the Kulin nation.

The most impacting message Mark has brought to the students was the importance of a right mindset and the influence of filters. Mark asked a group of students whether they view God through the filter of condemnation or grace, through the filter of forgiveness or retribution.

Suggesting if we view our faith through condemnation then subconsciously we'll anticipate messing up with the end result being punishment, and how we can even find skewed evidence in the Bible to feed this notion. Alternatively, Mark continued, if we have a foundational mindset saying *'we are never good enough'*, focusing on the mercy of God saving us by the skin-of-our-teeth, we'll develop a framework of survivalism; remaining forever thankful we've been saved, but never moving beyond this initial point of thankfulness due to a nervous heart robbing us of the freedom to attain the fullness of all God has for us.

Both of these mindsets hinder full freedom, the full inheritance and the rightful place that is inherently ours, whilst impacting our confidence to boast in Christ. The simple message as part of the cultural protocol was the importance of knowing our position as sons and daughters.

We can package God to be a God we're comfortable with, a recipe to Create-Our-Own-God based on the parts of God we like whilst downplaying or ignoring the parts we're confused by. A God where we can define his parameters, and a God who does not step outside of our comfort zone.

God is holy and God is righteous and our faith depends on God's holiness and righteousness. We need confidence in the one we call Lord and the one who'll provide eternal safety and protection. If God was not holy and was not righteous our future is not secure. God is love and God is good and God is the judge.

Chapter 32
God's Spiritual Compass

"Aslan is not a tame lion."

- Clyde S. Kilby [267]

No matter how hard I try, no matter what angle I take, regardless of how many arguments I've heard or read, I've failed to move from the simple truth that God is love. With this acting as my spiritual compass, I read the entirety of the Bible, including its contentious mysteries, and my faith remains intact.

God is love and there has to be an answer outside of love for all the bad things we hear about and read about. There is an answer, and it often takes time, discernment and faith to look at each story of the Bible, and the experiences and emotions we live through to reveal this love. Yet it's possible.

This book is centred on the philosophy that at the creation of humanity, at the start of our existence God declared his unconditional love for us. God proclaimed we are very good, and we bring joy to his life; the same joy experienced by parents at the birth of a child. Indescribable joy beyond words and God experienced this same joy with Adam and Eve. The language of words often leave a vacuum when describing emotions, yet we do have words to capture the relationship between God and humanity; 'very good'. God enjoyed fellowship with humanity and God was happy.

We then read how this relationship progressed; humanity fell and rejected God's love and chose an alternative deadly and destructive path. We broke love relationship and chose evil, yet God's love remained intact. Bible stories reveal the presence of evil, and the impact of evil is found in many stories of the Bible, both as a reminder of God's grace and mercy but also as warnings of choosing a wrong identity.

Chapter 33
The Dandelion Principle

"Once you have tasted flight, you will forever walk the earth with your eyes turned skyward, for there you have been, and there you will always long to return."

- Anonymous [268]

I dare myself to dream of a world where we became the catalytic world-changers we're called to be; gaining confidence in our identity, authority and empowered inheritance. Relying on the good reputation of God and being comfortable with sharing this reputation:

"All authority in heaven and on earth has been given to me. Therefore go."[269]

This global declaration resounds through the nations, and through the ages; Jesus has all authority, and he tells us to 'go' in the authority of heaven and earth:

"I have given you authority to trample on snakes and scorpions and to overcome all the power of the enemy; nothing will harm you."[270]

The redeeming work of Jesus is complete, and the transfer of authority to his sons and daughters fulfilled. James gives a compelling verdict on our new found spiritual inheritance:

"Submit yourselves, then, to God. Resist the devil, and he will flee from you."[271]

Is it any wonder the devil remains so intent on destroying our identity and robbing us of the full knowledge of God, whilst destroying God's reputation? We have the authority and we have the fullness of identity;

sons and daughters deeply loved by Abba.

Ruining our identity has to be a scheme of desperate survivalism for the devil:

- He could not defeat God at the rebellion
- He could not defeat God at the cross
- I doubt he has the audacity to face off against Holy Spirit, and
- With Heaven's authority now with his sons and daughters, he lives in fear of us realising our authority

He needs to destroy our identity and taint God's reputation.

I carry a picture in my heart of a dandelion (or 'lion's tooth' in its original French 'dent-de-lion' translation) and how this represents the birth and ministry of Jesus, the victory on the cross; the early Church, the arrival of Holy Spirit and the ongoing work of his children.

During its life cycle, the dent-de-lion develops a flower head; tiny clusters of individual flowers. Through apomixis the dent-de-lion produces seeds requiring no pollination, resulting in offspring genetically identical to the parent plant. Over a couple of days, the flower head dries out (giving the appearance of death) and is replaced by 'blowballs' or 'clocks'; the common name for its spherical seed-head.

We had hours of fun as kids, blowing these 'blowballs'; they represented parachutists, and with little effort, we could fill the environment with slow falling parachutes. The parachutes are actually fine hairs with seeds attached; their unique design and near weightlessness allow for an easy flight for countless seed over great distances. In the words of wiki they *"rapidly colonize disturbed soil."*[272]

The seed as a metaphor flows through the Bible; representing life, and growth. John captures this process:

"Very truly I tell you, unless a kernel of wheat falls to the ground and

dies, it remains only a single seed. But if it dies, it produces many seeds."[273]

The parallel of the dandelion and the life of Jesus are remarkable:

- Born through apomixes (Jesus was no ordinary baby)
- The 'lion's tooth' is from one shoot (Jesus descending from the Tribe of the Lion of Judah)
- A tight cluster of flowers is formed (the 12 Disciples)
- The flower dries out (the end of Jesus' public ministry, his arrest, trial and sentencing) giving the appearance of death over a couple of days (the cross and the tomb)
- Beyond death, seeds burst out ready to take flight (the early church and the arrival of Holy Spirit)
- Each seed represents the parent plant in identical genetic perfection (Jesus-believers being transformed into his likeness[274])

The devil may momentarily have taken delight at the drying up of the flower-head of Jesus, but his delight soon turned to dread as he witnessed the seed form a beautiful sphere (the early church). Dread turning to panic with the arrival of a breeze gently dislodging each seed to new territory (the promise of the Holy Spirit and the spread of God's love to the nations). A billion Jesus-people transformed to the likeness of Christ, spreading across the world, bringing a message of pure love and true identity.

To the devil, this must be terrifying.

We know we aren't Jesus, the devil knows we aren't Jesus, but the authority is the same. Mark writes:

"And these signs will accompany those who believe: In my name they will drive out demons; they will speak in new tongues; they will pick up snakes with their hands; and when they drink deadly poison, it will not hurt them at all; they will place their hands on sick people, and they will get well." [275]

Within my dandelion principle is simple instruction we do need to understand. Although we are not responsible for our existence, and we're not responsible for the natural growth process, we do have the capacity to hinder our spiritual development and the development of others. If we fail to reach spiritual maturity and remain in an infant state, we perhaps are not ready to be dispersed by the gentle breeze of Holy Spirit. We need a spiritual-kindergarten where our identities need further care and attention, and we need to grow in our understanding of God and his reputation. This is a safe place where we receive Abba's unconditional love but we are not ready for growth. Out of love for us, God withholds his plans and purposes for us until we are ready to be uprooted, dislodged and can thrive in hard soil where deep roots are needed so as we are not overpowered.

As mature Christians operating in full identity, we have the added responsibility for providing well tilled and fertile ground for others. This is discipleship and relationship.

Through a parable, Jesus teaches:

"Listen then to what the parable of the sower means: When anyone hears the message about the kingdom and does not understand it, the evil one comes and snatches away what was sown in their heart. This is the seed sown along the path. The seed falling on rocky ground refers to someone who hears the word and at once receives it with joy. But since they have no root, they last only a short time. When trouble or persecution comes because of the word, they quickly fall away. The seed falling among the thorns refers to someone who hears the word, but the worries of this life and the deceitfulness of wealth choke the word, making it unfruitful. But the seed falling on good soil refers to someone who hears the word and understands it. This is the one who produces a crop, yielding a hundred, sixty or thirty times what was sown." [276]

Chapter 34
Conclusion: Veil Free Living

This book aims to provoke our conscience, to consider God, and to determine the difference between the motivations of the leaders of the two kingdoms, to then use this knowledge as a spiritual compass when confronted with challenging situations.

Having confidence in God's good reputation and finding freedom in a healthy identity removes doubt, allowing us to reach a hurting world. It's an unfortunate situation right now in many countries where large pockets of the public see the church and her followers as hypocritical and meeting in out-dated institutions running contrary to social norms and popular culture.

God's light is a shadowless light with no room for shadows. Shadows appear when blockages get in the way. These blockages may be people, ideology, institutions, pressure groups etc. They cause a shadow and these shadows are where the devil lurks. We have not yet seen true light and true light will reveal the pure truth and pure holiness. We have shadows because we have many light sources, but there will be a day where there will be one eternal light source; [277] no more shadows, no more darkness, no more anything opposite to pure.

Our future is not necessarily fixed. In the big picture, the future is foretold and we know the promise of eternity. Yet for individual lives our futures are open, and this is where we add our ingredient of choice.

This mystery can keep God in the shadows. The devil thrives on misrepresenting God, whilst subtly encouraging us to question God to the point of accusation. He delights in taking security away from our identity, and shrouding the good reputation of God through a veil. He'll use scripture to confuse and enrage us; anything to remove us from the true identity of ourselves and the true reputation of God.

Do we believe the conquest of Canaan was all God's doing? That God devised the conquest, he planned for it and he executed it. Then what about us? God is the same God, he has not changed. The notion of the 'God of the Old Testament' is not a correct notion. Then maybe, just maybe, the chronic illness, the relational breakdown, the car crash, your friend's cancer, your spouse's redundancy, these just might be from God. As a litmus test, I'd offer a simple equation; if it comes from Heaven, it comes from God. [278] If there is no sickness in heaven, sickness does not come from God. If there is no pain in heaven, pain does not come from God. If there is no relational breakdown in heaven, then breakdown does not come from God.

Demographers tell me I'll live till I'm 80. That's fewer than 30,000 sunrises.

Under each sunrise I do not move from the position that my God is love, and my identity is secure in God's good reputation. Whereas the devil pushes an agenda of **doubt, fear** and **entitlement**; I live a life of **trust, faith** and **responsibility**. This is very attainable.

Bite-Sized Bible Study Guide

This guide recaps 12 main principles from the book, providing an opportunity to overview these principles in bite-sized chunks. It is intended for this guide to be used for purposes of reflection. Key quotes, themes, scriptures and challenges are provided for the 12-principles and the reader is encouraged to spend time on self-evaluation with an emphasis on developing a deeper love for God and facilitating the removal of barriers leading to a deeper intimacy with God.

The following sections will explore each of the following 12 principles:

Principle 1: The Character and Nature of Humans

Principle 2: Reputation and Identity

Principle 3: The Nine Spiritual Veils

Principle 4: Why People Suffer

Principle 5: The Character and Nature of God

Principle 6: God's Absence

Principle 7: The Character and Nature of Satan

Principle 8: The Manifestation of Satan's Failed Regime

Principle 9: Canaan, Propaganda & Earthly Government

Principle 10: The Manifestation of The Kingdom of God

Principle 11: The Struggle of Humanity

Principle 12: Freedom of Choice

PRINCIPLE 1
THE CHARACTER AND NATURE OF HUMANS

Key Quote:
Life's defining questions are centered on identity.

Key Theme:
We seek answers, seek to belong, and desire to know where we fit. We intrinsically sense something is out there and there's more to life than the natural eye can see.

Life's defining questions are centered on identity:
- Who am I?
- Where am I from?
- Why am I here?
- What should I do?
- Where am I going?

These questions are natural for us, and God is comfortable with our questions. We do, however, have the responsibility to ask these questions as a student rather than an accuser. When we're struggling to find answers to these questions we open ourselves to the potential of identity problems.

Key Scripture:
Jeremiah 29:11 (NIV): "For I know the plans I have for you," declares the LORD, "plans to prosper you and not to harm you, plans to give you hope and a future".

Key Challenge:
For the follower of Jesus, each of these questions has a general answer relevant for us all. However, there will also be specific answers for you personally. Spend time asking God to reveal his dreams for you, particularly on the questions of purpose ('Why am I here'?, and 'What should I do'?).

PRINCIPLE 2
REPUTATION AND IDENTITY

Key Quote:
Knowing God reveals our identity.

Key Theme:
There is a direct link between God and our identity. Knowing God reveals our identity, and knowing ourselves is critical as we navigate a hard and broken world. We hold an opinion on God, and this opinion becomes our personal reputation of God. When God's reputation is poor our identity suffers.

Unless we have confidence in God's reputation, and complete security in our identity, situations can dictate our future path.

The devil will try and taint God's reputation and mess with our identity through undermining God; telling lies, twisting the truth, causing confusion, and shaking our confidence. Leaving us with a growing sense of isolation, worthlessness, self-doubt, and self-pity. He sows seeds of doubt, we water them, and he watches them grow. It's no wonder so many of us struggle with identity and self-image.

We do not need to defend God, he speaks for himself, but we do need to present a true image of God allowing others to develop a relationship with him.

Key Scripture:
Ephesians 5:1 (ESV): Therefore be imitators of God.

Key Challenge:
Spend time with God, asking him to reveal any situations that are negatively impacting your walk with him. If God reveals any situations, ask God to remove them and to give you his strength to walk free of these situations. As part of this process, you may feel the conviction to ask for forgiveness.

PRINCIPLE 3
THE NINE SPIRITUAL VEILS

Key Quote:
It can become easy to lose sight of God whilst wearing a veil.

Key Theme:
This book introduces nine spiritual veils. The negative impact these veils have on our lives have been identified and names have been provided, grouped into:
- Doubt-based veils (Absent-God, Performance God)
- Fear-based veils (Karma-God, War-God, Angry-God, Schizophrenic-God)
- Entitlement-based veils (Happy-God, Genie-God, Safe-God)

We can package God to be a God we're comfortable with, a recipe to Create-Our-Own-God based on the parts of God we like whilst downplaying or ignoring the parts we're uncomfortable with. A God where we can define his parameters, based on our preferences.

We are too precious to have a veiled view of life, and a veiled view of God. It's the decisions we make, the actions we take, and the relationships we pursue under each sunrise that makes the difference.

It can become easy to lose sight of God whilst wearing a veil. It's during these times when we lose perspective we make poor decisions, and poor decisions so often result in deviations.

Instead of outwardly declaring *'holy, holy, holy'* from the fullness of identity, we focus inward and murmur a narrative of fear, doubt and entitlement creating a position of insecurity. Yet, this is not how our lives are meant to be. God desires for you and for me to become the best version of us that we can be. His dreams, his plans and his desires for us are beyond comprehension, they are unfathomably beautiful.

We need to identify the hurdles standing in the way of our identity.

Key Scripture:
2 Corinthians 3:16 (NIV): But whenever anyone turns to the Lord, the veil is taken away.

Key Challenge:
Reflect on your understanding of God. Do you have situations and questions causing you to doubt that God is always good and God is always loving? If so, pray to God and ask for his help in removing these areas that cause your doubt, freeing you to live in the fullness of God's love.

PRINCIPLE 4
WHY PEOPLE SUFFER

Key Quote:
Whatever we suffer, God suffered more, and he did this as a volunteer.

Key Theme:
'*Why does God allow suffering*' is a common question, merging together out-of-context components of understanding to form a wrong assumption; leading many to consider God as mean. We reach the flawed conclusion '*God is mean*' by using flawed arguments, flawed assumptions and flawed opinions.

The closeness of God to suffering can lead to accusations of God being the author of pain, and as there are no easy answers to why people suffer we may end up with more questions. The one thing we can be sure of, however; whatever we suffer, God suffered more, and he did this as a volunteer.

Key Scripture:
Isaiah 53:3-4 (NIV): He was despised and rejected by mankind, a man of suffering, and familiar with pain. Like one from whom people hide their faces he was despised, and we held him in low esteem. Surely he took up our pain and bore our suffering.

Key Challenge:
Are there areas in your life where you are holding a grudge against God for suffering that you blame Him for? These areas are often deep-rooted and may take considerable time to fully understand. Ask God to help you in this process and if areas of blame are highlighted ask God to heal these areas. In many instances, it is a good idea to share these areas with a trusted friend for support and prayer.

PRINCIPLE 5
THE CHARACTER AND NATURE OF GOD

Key Quote:
God loves us and God was pleased to create us.

Key Theme:
The origin of our story is simple; God loves us and God was pleased to create us. God went through the same life-changing amazement and sense of awe experienced by any new parent at the birth of their child. He called our family tree *'very good'*, and this is quite the compliment from the creator of the universe.

The Bible is the greatest romance ever told. The world's greatest love-story, of God, pursuing humanity through every page. We reject his love time and time again and prostitute ourselves with temptation. We ignore God, get angry with God, turn our backs on him, chase alternative lovers, generally ignore God and then blame God for the mess we've made. Yet, God remains relentless in his pursuit of us, costing Him the ultimate price through the death of Jesus. Jesus sheds undeniable light on God's character.

Key Scripture:
John 3:16 (NIV): For God so loved the world that he gave his one and only Son, that whoever believes in him shall not perish but have eternal life.

Key Challenge:
When you consider your inner-life, do you feel God's unconditional love? Are there areas of your life, and your memories where you do not feel this unconditional love? Spend time asking God to reveal barriers in your life where you may be shutting out God's unconditional love. God is a good God, he loves you unconditionally and he wants to bring healing and fullness.

PRINCIPLE 6
GOD'S ABSENCE

Key Quote:
God cannot be absent. Yet he can feel absent.

Key Theme:
Many of us do feel as though God is absent at times in our lives. God cannot be absent. Yet he can feel absent, and we can feel as though:
- God has withdrawn from us
- He's absent-minded when it comes to our particular needs
- He's forgotten us
- We're in a long-distance relationship with God
- He cares, but just not enough to show up on the day

We were never left alone, and we have never been without the ability to find God. When God is everywhere, yet he feels distant, we need to look at our own positioning.

Key Scripture:
Hebrews 13:5 (NIV): God has said, "Never will I leave you; never will I forsake you."

Key Challenge:
The way we relate to those who love us can sometimes be a reflection of the way in which we view God's relationship with us. Consider those you are close too, and review the 5-points above. Can you identify any of these 5 areas in your human relationships, and is this a reflection on the way you experience God's relationship with you?

PRINCIPLE 7
THE CHARACTER AND NATURE OF SATAN

Key Quote:
Satan operates in the shadows.

Key Theme:
Satan operates in the shadows. He deceives and promotes doubt, apathy, and poor self-worth to achieve his outcomes. He will use whatever it takes to block a true understanding of God and to filter our core belief in who God is. This will often be very subtle and will involve our identity. His tactics may not necessarily be to dissuade us of the existence of God; rather, spoil our view, and to make us unsure of our secure foundation.

Key Scripture:
John 8:44 (NIV): He was a murderer from the beginning, not holding to the truth, for there is no truth in him. When he lies, he speaks his native language, for he is a liar and the father of lies.

Key Challenge:
When considering your routines, choices and habits, are there times where you conduct your life in '*a shadow*', out of sight from people? There is a difference between privacy and secrecy. Life does require differing levels of privacy, yet there are very few times in life where we should be in secrecy. Reflect on your life and consider if you are spending time in the shadows of secrecy. If so, ask God to help you and to bring freedom.

PRINCIPLE 8
THE MANIFESTATION OF SATAN'S FAILED REGIME

Key Quote:
We learned new ways to deal with the emotions and desires we were never created to cope with.

Key Theme:
At Eden, we learned nomadic wandering. Yet we were never left alone. The face-to-face intimate relationship with God had become a distant notion, to be fully restored in the future, yet remained shrouded in mystery.

The relationship between man and woman became strained and the relationship between humankind and God became confused. As this relational gap deepened and became more complex, we learned new ways to deal with the emotions and desires we were never created to cope with (greed, lust, pride, insecurity, pain, failure and hurt to name a few) and the physical actions these emotions and desires lead to (break-up, isolation, anxiety, violence, and divorce).

Through sin, we became exposed to the knowledge of evil. We began to understand evil without the self-capacity to withstand evil. At this point everything changed for humanity, we became vulnerable and needy. Yet, nothing changed for God. Adam and Eve were removed from Paradise and continued the human species, passing on from one generation to the next this exposure to evil.

Evil established a beach-head for the Kingdom of Darkness. In the 21st Century, this failed regime breeds through war, slavery, illness, and suffering whilst robbing our most basic human need: the fullness of relationship with Abba. By robbing this human need, our identity searches for an elusive anchor and soon we become imprisoned by fake identity.

We can downplay the seriousness of personal sin in our lives and develop a false sense of safety by using the changing benchmark of societal norms to determine our own level of personal behaviour; where (for example) society doesn't consider gossip, or greed as all that bad these days, and pornography can simply become a personal freedom of choice. God has not changed and the gap between the benchmark he has called us to and the general state of many societies widens year after year.

Key Verse:
James 1:15 (NIV): Then, after desire has conceived, it gives birth to sin; and sin, when it is full-grown, gives birth to death.

Key Challenge:
As humans, we do not operate out of instinct but we respond from a spiritual reality. Reflect on your reactions to everyday situations; are these Godly responses reflecting the fruit of the Spirit (Gal 5:22-23); or, do our reactions reflect an undercurrent of insecurity reflecting the principles of rejection or rebellion?

PRINCIPLE 9
CANAAN, PROPAGANDA & EARTHLY GOVERNMENT

Key Quote:
Canaan was a tragedy, but it was an avoidable tragedy, and this is the key to understanding Canaan.

Key Theme:
Satan deploys propaganda to entice and destabilize. When we doubt our identity we may fail to identify the difference between truth and propaganda. When this happens, the enemy has gained a foothold in a person's life. When society fails to see this difference, the enemy has established a beach-head at the heart of society.

When the principles of heaven's government are reflected on earth, the community is developed and strengthened. Without heaven's dynamic, world governments operate on a continuum of achieving good results through to delivering harsh systems of control. Earthly governments can become so intent on hatred they open themselves to the dreadful specter of Satan's influence. History shows many governments had a strong ideology, but dreadful values.

The conquest of Canaan remains a reference point for many who look to discredit God and accuse God of anything other than 'love'; God invites us on a journey of discovery to investigate Canaan and provides all the information we need to form a conclusion. We do not remove God from the equation of Canaan, but we do need to understand the equation and form the right question.

Canaan was a tragedy, but it was an avoidable tragedy, and this is the key to understanding Canaan.

Key Scripture:
Genesis 1:27, 31 (NIV): So God created mankind in his own image, in the image of God he created them; male and female he created them…God saw all that he had made, and it was very good.

Key Challenge:
Joshua's conquest of Canaan is amongst the most contentious of Biblical narratives. Yet, Canaan was an avoidable tragedy. In your personal life, are there areas that you feel are out-of-control? Areas that keep you up at night and rob you of needed sleep? Areas that seem like a downward spiral with no pause button. It is for these very reasons that Jesus came to rescue us. Spend some time asking God to reveal areas that may be out-of-control (these could be financial, relational, career etc.).

PRINCIPLE 10
THE MANIFESTATION OF THE KINGDOM OF GOD

Key Quote:
Jesus voluntarily experienced every emotion, fear, doubt, temptation, and humiliation common to humanity.

Key Theme:
Jesus, as the full representation of God on earth, became our reference point for all who God is; the unveiled view of God.

Jesus humbled himself and entered our human existence as a naked human baby; totally dependent, totally vulnerable, and needing protection from his human parents. Jesus voluntarily experienced every emotion, fear, doubt, temptation, and humiliation common to humanity.

Key Scripture:
Philippians 2:6-8 (NIV): Who, being in very nature God, did not consider equality with God something to be used to his own advantage; rather, he made himself nothing by taking the very nature of a servant, being made in human likeness. And being found in appearance as a man, he humbled himself by becoming obedient to death—even death on a cross!

Key Challenge:
Jesus understands us, and His empathy towards us is unquestionable. Jesus knows us because he lived as one of us and experienced every trial and temptation. Are there burdens in your life that you've never asked God to remove, or burdens that seem to repeat themselves and you feel as though you are on a round-a-bout without the ability to find freedom? God is right there with you, he knows you intimately and desires to free you. Jesus longs to hear you ask for his help to bring freedom to all areas of your life.

PRINCIPLE 11
THE STRUGGLE OF HUMANITY

Key Quote:
You're not good enough, you need more, you need to look different, you don't fit in, attain self-sufficiency, control your own destiny and make a name for yourself.

Key Theme:
We are influenced by two narratives of life:
1. God's narrative; you are loved, you are wanted, you are pure and you are special
2. Satan's counter-narrative; you're not good enough, you need more, you need to look different, you don't fit in, attain self-sufficiency, control your own destiny and make a name for yourself

The devil thrives on misrepresenting God, whilst subtly encouraging us to question God to the point of accusation. He delights in taking security away from our identity and shrouding the good reputation of God through a veil.

The devil pushes an agenda of doubt, fear and personal entitlement; where we have been redeemed for a life of faith, assurance and spiritual increase.

Key Scripture:
2 Corinthians 3:18 (NIV): And we all, who with unveiled faces contemplate the Lord's glory, are being transformed into his image with ever-increasing glory, which comes from the Lord, who is the Spirit.

Key Challenge:
Many live in cultures where pride and making a name for ourselves is celebrated. Being able to develop to our full-potential is actually a gift from God; however, when we put the emphasis on human achievement we take the personal glory and God can be rejected. In reviewing our societies, which is the most evident: celebrating human achievement or celebrating

God's gifts to humanity? How can you demonstrate a life of giving glory to God in all circumstances; to take the spotlight away from personal glory and humbly acknowledge God?

PRINCIPLE 12
FREEDOM OF CHOICE

Key Quote:
Freedom is not possible without Christ.

Key Theme:
Freedom of choice is a decision God took; giving creation the ability to turn their back on their creator. Many see engagement with Christianity as the giving up of rights and freedom and replacing these with ritual and sacrifice. However, freedom is not possible without Christ. Even in the most democratic of nations, we do not have complete freedom.

Key Scripture:
Galatians 5:13-14 (NIV): You, my brothers and sisters, were called to be free. But do not use your freedom to indulge the flesh; rather, serve one another humbly in love. For the entire law is fulfilled in keeping this one command: "Love your neighbor as yourself."

Key Challenge:
The difference between rights and freedom may not always be clear, and the holding on to personal rights may mean we miss out on the fullness of freedom in God. Spend some time reflecting on areas of your life where your rights might be jeopardizing your true freedom in Christ. For example, many of us live in democracies where you have the right to engage in activity that runs contrary to the principles of the kingdom of God. You have the right to retain every penny and cent you earn and not consider the plight of the poor; yet, freedom in God would lead us to care for the poor and down-trodden. We may live in nations where we have the right to emotionally disconnect from those around us; yet, this runs contrary to values of community in the Kingdom of Heaven.

References

1. Norman Maclean. *A River Runs Through It and Other Stories.* University of Chicago Press: 1976.
2. Genesis 3:16-19 NIV
3. 1 John 2:2 NIV
4. Hebrews 2:14-18 NIVUK
5. The Book of Joshua NIV
6. Proverbs 25:2 NIV
7. Malachi 1:2-3 CJB
8. Bill Bryson. *The Lost Continent: Travels in Small Town America.* p13. Harper & Row: 1989.
9. Bill Bryson *The Lost Continent: Travels in Small Town America.* p14. Harper & Row: 1989.
10. Joel 2 NIVUK
11. Joel 2:2 NIVUK
12. Joel 2:25 NIV
13. Queensland tourism slogan
14. Lamentations 3:22-23 ESV
15. Hebrews 3:13 NIV
16. Lamentations 3:22-23 NIV
17. Ephesians 4:26 NIV
18. Attributed to Robert Burns, *Collected Poems of Robert Burns*
19. Colossians 1:13 NIV
20. Colossians 1:13 NIV
21. Lewis Carroll. *Alice's Adventures in Wonderland.* Chapter 6. Macmillan: 1865.
22. Hebrews 5:9 NIV
23. John 8:44 NIV
24. 1 Corinthians 14:10-11 CJB
25. 2 Corinthians 3:18 NIVUK
26. John Maxwell, http://hillsong.com/conference/blog/2016/05/john-maxwell-hsc30-connect/#.V5Ve9qLzByE), accessed September 2016.
27. Colossians 1:26-27 NIV
28. Romans 12:2 NIVUK
29. Psalm 139:7-10 NIVUK

30. Galatians 3:1-3 NIVUK
31. Romans 8:35-39; Ephesians 2:8-9 NIVUK
32. Genesis 1:26 NIVUK
33. *(Intentionally Blank)*
34. Revelation 12:7 NIVUK
35. Leo Tolstoy. *War and Peace.* The Russian Messenger, 1869.
36. Job 1:6; Matthew 4:1 NIV
37. Romans 8:22 NIVUK
38. Romans 8:18-23 NIVUK
39. *Matthew Henry's Commentary on the Whole Bible Volume 6.* Acts to Revelation, verse Acts 8:18-25. 1706.
40. Genesis 1:27 NIVUK
41. Matthew 27:46 NIVUK
42. Genesis 4:8; 10-12 NIVUK
43. Revelation 1:14 NIVUK
44. Abraham Maslow. *Psychological Review: A Theory of Human Motivation.* 50 (4): 370–96. American Psychological Association (United States): 1943.
45. Harriet Beecher Stowe. *Uncle Tom's Cabin.* Boston: John P. Jewett & Co, 1852.
46. iMDB. End of the World Apocalyptic Disaster Films and movies which I have seen, http://www.imdb.com/list/ls009625336/, accessed September 2016.
47. Matthew 11:12 NIVUK
48. Ephesians 6:10-20 NIVUK
49. Joel 2:11 NIVUK
50. 2 Timothy 3:1-5 The Message
51. guinnessworldrecords.com - Best-selling book of non-fiction http://www.guinnessworldrecords.com/world-records/best-selling-book-of-non-fiction/ , accessed September 2016
52. Joel 2:1-2 NIVUK
53. Acts 2:17 NIVUK
54. Acts 2:17-21 NIVUK
55. Acts 2:19-20 NIVUK
56. Revelation 6:1-8 NIVUK
57. Ecclesiastes 1:2 NIVUK
58. Michelle Magorian. *Goodnight Mister.* Tom Kestrel Books, 1981
59. Michelle Magorian. *Goodnight Mister.* Tom Kestrel Books, 1981
60. 2 Samuel 11:14 NIV

61. Matthew 1:6 NIVUK
62. Psalm 51:1-2 ESV
63. Anne Frank. http://www.annefrankonline.com/ , accessed September 2016
64. Kurt Vonnegut. *Slaughterhouse-Five*. pp 74-75. Dell Publishing, 1969.
65. Aesop. The Dog and the Shadow, http://www.bartleby.com/17/1/3.html, accessed September 2016
66. *Managing Business Ethics. Straight Talk About How To Do It Right.* 4th Edition, Cram101 Textbook Reviews, 2016
67. *Daily Mail*. "Do YOU post a selfie every day and constantly worry about comments on it?" Take the test that can reveal if you're a 'like addict' http://www.dailymail.co.uk/sciencetech/article-3528993/Do-post-selfie-day-constantly-worry-comments-test-reveal-like-addict.html, accessed Septmber 2016
68. Royal Children's Hospital Melbourne. Youth Suicide in Australia: http://www.rch.org.au/cah/research/Youth_Suicide_in_Australia/ , accessed Septmeber 2016
69. 2 Corinthians 3:16 NIVUK
70. Pope Francis. *Lumen Fidei: Encyclical letter Lumen Fidei Pope Francis, Lumen Fidei: Enciclica sulla Fede*, http://www.basilicadelamerce.com/blog-en/Lumen-Fidei-34.html , accessed September 2016.
71. *(Intentionally Blank)*
72. Joseph Matthews, 2016
73. C. S. Lewis. *The Magicians Nephew*. p123. The Bodley Head, 1955.
74. Genesis 1:31 NIVUK
75. Deuteronomy 20:16-17 NIVUK
76. Genesis 1:31 NIV
77. John 10:10 NIV
78. John 10:10 NIV
79. Philip Yancey. *Rumors of Another World: What on Earth Are We Missing?* Zondervan, 2003.
80. Anaïs Nin. *Risk*. http://www.poemhunter.com/poem/risk/ , accessed September 2016.
81. John 10:10 NIV
82. *Animal Structure and Function Volume 5*, 12th Edition Cram101, 2014.
83. Dictionary.com. *Segue* -http://www.dictionary.com/browse/segue , accessed September 2016.
84. Lenny LeBlanc. *There is None Like You*, Integrity's Hosanna! Music, 1991.

85. Gene Edwards. *The Divine Romance*. Tyndale House Publishers, 1992.
86. Gen 6:5-6; Isaiah 53:3 NIV
87. Ezekiel 6:9 and Psalm 95:10 NIV
88. John 11:38 NIV
89. John 11:3 NIV
90. Psalm 78:38; Isaiah 12:1, Psalm 78:58 NIV
91. Micah 7:18-19 NIV
92. Zephaniah 3:17 NIV
93. Proverbs 24:12 NIV
94. Isaiah 5:26; Zechariah 10:8 NIV
95. Zechariah 1:14-15 NIV
96. Exodus 32:14; Jeremiah 26:19; Amos 7:3 NIV
97. Nicholas Matthews 2016
98. Papal Encyclicals Online. *Confronting the Devil's Power Address of Pope Paul VI to a General Audience November 15, 1972.* Papal Encyclicals Online, http://www.papalencyclicals.net/Paul06/p6devil.htm , accessed September 2016.
99. Papal Encyclicals Online. *Confronting the Devil's Power Address of Pope Paul VI to a General Audience November 15, 1972.* Papal Encyclicals Online, http://www.papalencyclicals.net/Paul06/p6devil.htm , accessed September 2016.
100. Papal Encyclicals Online. *Confronting the Devil's Power Address of Pope Paul VI to a General Audience November 15, 1972.* Papal Encyclicals Online, http://www.papalencyclicals.net/Paul06/p6devil.htm , accessed September 2016.
101. Romans 6:23 NIV
102. Richard Attenborough. http://www.goodreads.com/quotes/362111-there-is-a-light-in-this-world-a-healing-spirit , accessed September 2016.
103. Isaiah 53:2-6 The Message
104. Kasher and Witztum. *King Herod: A Persecuted Persecutor*. p12. Walter de Gruyter GmbH, 2007.
105. Jamey Heit. *The Politics of the Hunger Games.* pg 1. McFarland & Company Inc. 2015
106. wikipedia.org, *Massacre_of_the_Innocents* https://en.wikipedia.org/wiki/Massacre_of_the_Innocents#cite_note-28 , accessed September 2016.
107. Deuteronomy 22:20-21; Numbers 5:11-31 NIV

108. Luke 4:28 ESV
109. Philippians 2:6-8 NIVUK
110. Mark 3:21 NIVUK
111. John 7:5 NIVUK
112. Luke 13:1 NIVUK
113. Revelation 5:4 NIVUK
114. Revelation 5:6 NIVUK
115. Revelation 5:6 NIVUK
116. Philippians 2:6-8 NIV
117. Billy Graham. *Why Easter Matters* https://billygraham.org/story/why-easter-matters-10-billy-graham-quotes/ , accessed September 2016.
118. Matthew 16:14 NIVUK
119. Matthew 16:14 NIVUK
120. Matthew 16: 15-16 NIVUK
121. Philippians 2:6 NIVUK
122. John 3:16 NIVUK
123. 1 John 3:16 NIVUK
124. 1 John 4:8 NIVUK
125. Corinthians 13:4-8 NIV
126. Jim Steinman. *I'd Do Anything for Love (But I Won't Do That)*, 1993.
127. Isaiah 53:2-5 NIVUK
128. Isaiah 53:7-8 NIVUK
129. Exodus 34:6-7 NIVUK
130. Exodus 33:7 NIVUK
131. Exodus 33:11 NIVUK
132. Genesis 3:8 NIVUK
133. Numbers 6:25 NIVUK
134. 1 Corinthians 13:12 NIVUK
135. Exodus 32:16 NIVUK
136. Exodus 34:6-7 NIVUK
137. Exodus 34:7 NIVUK
138. Galatians 5:22-23 NIVUK
139. 1 Corinthians 12:7-10 NIV
140. Galatians 5:23 NIVUK
141. Psalm 14:2 NIVUK
142. Joyce Meyer. *Who Is God* (Part 6). Rhema FM, 2016.
143. C.S. Lewis. *Mere Christianity.* Geoffrey Bles, 1952.

144. Isaiah 55:8-9 NIVUK
145. Isaiah 7:14-15 NIV
146. Luke 2:40 NIV
147. Hebrews 5:7-10 NIVUK
148. Fyodor Dostoyevsky. Quoted by Jürgen Moltman, Science and Wisdom, in John Wilson, The Best Christian Writing, 170-71. Harper San Francisco, 2002.
149. mathforum.org, *The Missing Dollar*, http://mathforum.org/dr.math/faq/faq.missing.dollar.html , accessed September 2016.
150. John 1:1-2; 14a NIVUK
151. 2 Peter 3:13 NIV
152. Revelation 21:4 NIVUK
153. C.S. Lewis. *The Magician's Nephew*. The Bodley Head, 1955.
154. Leo Tolstoy. *War and Peace*. The Russian Messenger, 1869.
155. Genesis 15:16; Leviticus 18:21-30; 20:2-5; Deuteronomy 12:29-31; etc NIV
156. Winston Churchill. *The Second World War Volume 1: The Gathering Storm*. pg 64. Houghton Mifflin Company, 1948.
157. Revelation 7:9 NIVUK
158. John 3:16 NIVUK
159. Ezekiel 28:12-18 NIVUK
160. Papal Encyclicals Online. *Confronting the Devil's Power Address of Pope Paul VI to a General Audience November 15, 1972*. Papal Encyclicals Online, http://www.papalencyclicals.net/Paul06/p6devil.htm , accessed September 2016.
161. Genesis 3:15 NIVUK
162. Various, During the trial of Jesus NIV
163. Matthew 27:11-14; Mark 15:1-5; Luke 23:1-4, 9; John 18:33-38 NIV
164. Footnote: Noah, Shem, Ham, Japheth and their wives (Genesis 7:13) NIV
165. Genesis 15:19-21 NIV
166. Footnote: Kenites, Kenizzites, Kadmonites, Hittites, Perizzites, Rephaites, Amorites, Canaanites, Girgashites and Jebusites (Genesis 15:19-21) NIV
167. Genesis 15:18-21 NIV
168. Deuteronomy 1:8 NIV
169. Genesis 28:13 NIV
170. Deuteronomy 1:8 NIV

171. Exodus 12:48; 20:10; 22:21 NIV
172. Exodus 22:21 NIV
173. Exodus 22:21; Exodus 23:9 NIV
174. Exodus 12:49 NIV
175. Leviticus 19:33-34 NIV
176. Exodus 20:10 NIV
177. Deuteronomy 16:14 NIV
178. Numbers 15:27-29; Lev 17:8-9; Numbers 15:14-16; 19:10 NIV
179. Leviticus 16:29 NIV
180. Exodus 12:48-49 NIV
181. Genesis 12:6 NIVUK
182. Genesis 21:34; 23:7; 23:20 NIV
183. Genesis 12:5; 13:1-4 NIV
184. Genesis 15:6; Romans 4:1-3 NIV
185. Genesis 10 NIV
186. Matthew Henry. *Matthew Henry's Commentary on the Whole Bible.* Volume 6, Acts to Revelation, verse Acts 17:26. 1706.
187. Genesis 1:26-31 NIVUK
188. Psalm 136:1-2 NIV
189. Hebrews 13:8 NIV
190. Genesis 4:6-7 NIVUK
191. Chris Bruno. *The Whole Story of the Bible in 16 Verses.* Crossway Books, 2015.
192. Deuteronomy 4:9 NIVUK NIVUK
193. Genesis 15:12-16 NIV
194. Matthew Henry. *Matthew Henry's Commentary on the Whole Bible.* Volume 1, Genesis to Deuteronomy, verses Exodus 13:17-22; Exodus 13:17-18. 1706.
195. Exodus 13:18 ESV
196. Exodus 13:17 NIVUK
197. Numbers 14:13-14 NIVUK
198. Isaiah 55:11 NIV
199. Exodus 14:21 NIV
200. Joshua 3:16 KJV
201. Matthew 1:5-6 NIVUK
202. Herbert Lockyer. *All the Women of the Bible.* p131. Zondervan, 1961.
203. Leo Tolstoy. *War and Peace.* The Russian Messenger, 1869.
204. Hebrews 7:2 NIVUK

205. Hebrews 7:2 NIVUK
206. Hebrews 7:2 NIVUK
207. Genesis 32:22-30 NIV
208. Joshua 5:13-15 NIVUK
209. Daniel 3:25 KJB
210. Isaiah 28:15-19 NIVUK
211. Colossians 2:13 NIVUK
212. Joshua 5:1 NIVUK
213. Joshua 2:2 NIVUK
214. Matthew 2:1-5 NIVUK
215. Joshua 2:9-11 NIVUK
216. Joshua 2:24 NIVUK
217. Joshua 6:1; NASB
218. Isaiah 17:9 NIVUK
219. Matthew Henry. *Matthew Henry's Commentary on the Whole Bible.* Volume 1, Genesis to Deuteronomy, verse Leviticus 18:28. 1706.
220. 1 Corinthians 13:4-5 NIVUK
221. Richard Dawkins. *The God Delusion.* p51. Mariner Books, 2008.
222. Bill Bullard. http://www.goodreads.com/quotes/573919-opinion-is-really-the-lowest-form-of-human-knowledge-it , accessed September 2016.
223. Matthew Champion. *What Stephen Fry would say if he met God.* https://www.indy100.com/article/what-stephen-fry-would-say-if-he-met-god--gk01sclnie , accessed September 2016.
224. 2 Peter 2:5 NIVUK
225. Genesis 6:5 NIV
226. Genesis 6:3 NIV
227. Gregory A. Boyd. *Repenting of Religion: Turning from Judgment to the Love of God.* p135. Baker, 2004.
228. Matthew 15:28 NIVUK
229. Mark 10:46 NIV
230. Luke 19:9 NIV
231. Ecclesiastes 3:1 NIVUK
232. see 1 Chronicles 21:13 NIV
233. Ecclesiastes 3:11 NIV
234. A.W. Tozer (compiled and edited by James L. Snyder). *And He Dwelt Among Us: Teachings from the Gospel of John.* p47. Bethany House, 2009.
235. *BBC World News America.*

https://archive.org/details/WHYY_20140717_233000_BBC_World_News_America , accessed September 2016.

236. Genesis 3:22 NIVUK
237. Revelation 9:6 NIVUK
238. John 12:24 NIV
239. The Book of Jonah NIV
240. Genesis 6-8 NIV
241. Steven Moffat. *The Dr Dances Season 1, Episode 10.* 2006.
242. http://www.telegraph.co.uk. *Dr Who Daleks 'more familiar to children than real animals'* http://www.telegraph.co.uk/news/earth/earthnews/3346635/Dr-Who-Daleks-more-familiar-to-children-than-real-animals.html , accessed September 2016.
243. https://en.wikipedia.org, *History of Doctor Who* https://en.wikipedia.org/wiki/History_of_Doctor_Who , accessed September 2016.
244. C.S. Lewis. *The Screwtape Letters.* Geoffrey Bles, 1942.
245. Paul Simon. *You Can Call Me Al,* 1986.
246. Philippians 3:20 NIV
247. Fiona Macrae. *Were you BORN to be single? Scientists discover a gene that makes certain people bad at relationships.* The Daily Mail. 21 November 2014.
248. Captain EJ Smith (Captain of the Titanic)
249. 2 Kings 17:7-17; Matthew 21:33-46 NIV
250. 2 Kings 22 NIV
251. Acts 17:28 NIVUK
252. Luke 19:41-44 NIVUK
253. UK Apologetics. *Jerusalem, AD70: The Worst Desolation Ever?* http://www.ukapologetics.net/09/AD70.htm , accessed September 2016.
254. Steve Maraboli. http://www.goodreads.com/quotes/336992-a-broken-heart-bleeds-tears , accessed September 2016.
255. 1 Corinthians 13 NIV
256. 2 Peter 3:9 NIV
257. C.S. Lewis. *Prince Caspian.* Geoffrey Bles, 1951.
258. Micah 6:8 NIV
259. Joel 2:13-14 NIVUK
260. Dr Bhatia. *Textbook on Legal Language and Legal Writing.* Universal Law Publishing Co PVT Ltd, 2010.
261. Hosea 13:14; 1 Corinthians 15:55-57; Galatians 3:13 NIV

262. Bob Geldof, Midge Ure. *Do They know It's Christmas Time*, 1984.
263. *(Intentionally Blank)*
264. John 14:12 NIVUK
265. Revelation 4:8 NIVUK
266. A. W. Tozer. *The Knowledge of the Holy*. San Francisco: Harper Collins 1961
267. Clyde S. Kilby. *The Christian World of C. S. Lewis*. p136. William B. Eerdmans Publishing Company, 1964.
268. Anonymous, some suggest Leonardo da Vinci
269. Matthew 28:18-19a NIVUK
270. Luke 10:19 NIVUK
271. James 4:7 NIVUK
272. https://en.wikipedia.org. *Taraxacum*. https://en.wikipedia.org/wiki/Taraxacum , accessed September 2016.
273. John 12:24 NIVUK
274. 2 Corinthians 3:18, Colossians 3:10 NIV
275. Mark 16:17-18 NIVUK
276. Matthew 13:18-23 NIVUK
277. Revelation 21:23 NIV
278. Matthew 6:10 NIV

About the Author

Originally from the UK, Nicholas Matthews has lived, worked in and travelled throughout Africa, Asia, Europe and the Pacific.

In recent years Nicholas has been leading schools where students are encouraged to discover and practice their faith in the classroom and on mission.

With 20 years of full time volunteer work he's seen first-hand many of the challenges of this world and his faith persuades him there is an answer.

Nicholas now resides in Melbourne Australia with his wife, Sarah, and two sons. He works full-time for YWAM.

For More Information

For more information concerning Nicholas Matthews, Billy Hallowell, or St. Polycarp Publishing House, please visit the following sites:

Nicholas Matthews

Web: https://www.amazon.com/Nik-Matthews/e/B01MYCK7K8
Facebook: @30Ksunrises
Instagram: @30k_sunrises
Twitter: @30k_sunrises

Billy Hallowell

Web: https://www.pathufind.com
Facebook: @billyhallowell
Instagram: @billyhallowell
Twitter: @BillyHallowell

St. Polycarp Publishing House

Web: https://stpolycarppublishinghouse.com
Facebook: @stpolycarppublishing
Instagram: @stpolycarppublishinghouse
Twitter: @StPolycarpPub

The Nine Veils

www.ingramcontent.com/pod-product-compliance
Lightning Source LLC
Chambersburg PA
CBHW060603230426
43670CB00011B/1941